"Anyone who loves  ...ny
and well worth taking ...u.

—Warren Eckstein, syndicated radio host of The Pet Show
and author of "How To Get Your Dog To Do What You Want"

"Ms. Zola writes of the odyssey she and her husband took with her
'Lifetime Dog,' Mr. Chips, with humor, affection, curiosity, love &
deep devotion. You will laugh and cry and hopefully learn from
this very touching account of a true human-animal bond."

—Ila Davis, DVM, PhD., DACVIM, Veterinarian For Monterey
County and City of Salinas Animal Services.

"High Paws to a 'Pawsitively' wonderfully written book about the
life of a rescue dog. A must read for all dog lovers. Especially me."

—Nancy Sarnoff, President, Perfect Pet Rescue.

"Sensitive and touching. Each page is filled with the fun and
satisfaction of living with and saving the life of a shelter dog. It
reminds me of the joy I experienced, the appreciation and love I
received from my own two shelter adoptions."

—Elliot Katz, DVM, President Emeritus, In Defense of Animals

Romancing the Dog

THE STRUGGLE TO MAKE A POUND DOG HAPPY IN BEVERLY HILLS

MARION ZOLA

Front Cover Photo by Ted Goldstein

ISBN: 0615584861
ISBN-13: 9780615584867
Library of Congress Control Number:
2011946272
Planet Publishing, Beverly Hills, CA

FOR ALL THE DOGS AND CATS
IN SHELTERS EVERYWHERE
WHO NEVER GOT ADOPTED

TABLE OF CONTENTS

PROLOGUE

"I'm never getting married again," my blind date told me in a dimly lit, elegant Italian restaurant. Sam had separated from his first wife just four months earlier. During a good part of the dinner that followed I heard all about the Poodle left behind at his former house. Although a quiet man, he grew animated, proud as he spoke of Daisy's cleverness at distinguishing her toys by name, her prowess at hide'n'seek, and habit of sleeping under the covers on her back, with her paws crossed, exactly as he did with his hands. "She knew her hamburger from her hot dog and bone by name." Sam had even taken Daisy to wine tastings when he lived in Carmel, on the California central coast, where wineries are abundant in the area.

"She prefers burgundies to Bordeaux," he announced with a perfectly straight face. "And she absolutely rejects champagnes." Clearly, this guy loved his dog. Having always been an "animal person" I was impressed, character revealing itself in such offerings. The aging Daisy's deafness and poor eyesight made it difficult to remove her from the home she was used to, which Sam's ex kept. So the Miniature Poodle had gone the way of his first marriage. Taking her with him would have been a problem compounded by Sam's traveling every week, from L.A., where he now lived, to Palo Alto where he worked. After thirteen years of living with Daisy, he truly regretted having to leave her behind. "Best dog I ever had," he said sadly.

After we dated a while, I suggested that Sam reclaim Daisy, who had really been *his* dog, and that I care for her while he was out of town. Being a writer, I work at home and would have been with her most of the time. But this never happened. Daisy only got occasional weekend visits with her dad. Eventually, she died of a heart attack.

One weekend after we'd been dating almost four years Sam gave me a three inch tall frog prince sculpture complete with crown and "diamond" ring in his hand. This was to indicate that he'd changed his mind about marriage. The wedding was the following year. Our long courtship and early married life made for nine happy but dogless years of work and travel. We moved to Beverly Hills, a strange iconic sort of place for a former Westside Manhattanite to land. Sam touted the neighborhood's superb police and fire services, two advantages I hoped never to avail myself of.

On walks in the area we always stopped to pet OPD - other people's dogs – and naturally began thinking of getting our own. People have fantasies about pets, like they do about children. We'll do this with them and that – I summoned up visions of Frisbee and ball games in the yard with an exuberantly happy and independent dog, nights by the fire with Sam and I reading, the pooch playing with his latest toy. Vacations would be no problem. We'd pop him or her into a doggy camp we'd heard about. All the built in joy of outdoor life among similarly privileged pets had to be nirvana. By now, Sam worked more and more at home, not needing to be at his office as often. With both of us at home, having a dog seemed like a snap. And with Sam's company winding down, he only went to the office in Northern California for a few days now and then.

I wanted to make sure that we adopted a homeless dog, any one whose life was at risk. After all, over four to six million a year are put to death just because there's no one to give them a home. Sam clearly yearned for another Daisy. Like most people, he wanted a dog like the one he'd already known and loved. Given our separate requirements meant finding a homeless female Miniature Poodle. How hard could that be?

Chapter 1

THE POODLE WHO WASN'T

I like a bit of mongrel myself, whether it's a man or a dog; they're the best for every day.

GEORGE BERNARD SHAW

My first call was to Poodle Rescue. They had only one Miniature available at the moment. We went and encountered a nervous, strange looking dog. Nothing clicked with him. But there were others around town. During our first superficial search, we encountered a few different sized Poodles, partial Poodles, very-little-part Poodle combos, but no actual Miniature Poodle. We even met a tiny three-legged dynamo, mostly

Chihuahua, born that way, whom Sam immediately felt had no chance at adoption except with us.

"Here's our number," he said, handing the rescue person at the facility a piece of paper. "If no one wants him, we'll take the little guy."

He's not a Poodle! I feel like shouting but don't. Stunned, I realize at this instant that Sam's Poodle resolve is not set in stone; that he's first and foremost an animal lover. Fortunately, his prediction about the three legged dog turned out to be wrong. A young couple looking at him while we're there finds the little hopper mesmerizing. Checking later, we discover that they have adopted him.

We jump from one rescue place to another but haven't met the right dog yet. Then I get a call from Perfect Pet Rescue, in our neighborhood. Nancy, who runs it, was on the other end.

"I just brought a grey, female Miniature Poodle to the hospital. Why don't you check her out?" She sounds like exactly what we're looking for. I go, I see and call Nancy from there.

"The dog seems just fine, but Sam won't be back until after two o'clock. He has to see her." Nancy also wants me to take a look at the "black and white Poodle mix" in a cage at the back of the pet hospital.

There I find a curled up, black and white mutt in an outside cage. Appearing nothing at all like a Poodle, the skinny fellow she calls a "Poodle mix" had been brought in for cleaning up from the pound a few days before. As I approach the cage, he growls. I take off my sun visor and sunglasses, bend down and say a few friendly words.

The dog immediately put his paws on the cage in the most supplicating gesture, and stares penetratingly into my eyes. What a look! The tail moves ever so slightly from side to side. This was it. Love at first sight. He has let me know him, see into his soul, and we have bonded. Would I turn away? He was counting on me, his intelligent eyes said. I remember a very old lady we once met who told me that "when you find the right pet, you just know it." This was surely the boy for me. But what of my promise to Sam? Surely his trust in me would be gone if I tossed the Poodle commitment out the window?

The little caged guy, a solid medium size, all black and white irregular patches, had a striking haphazard design, and sported large, mostly white paws. His face, in contrast to his body, came out perfectly symmetrical – a white mouth and mustache leading to a black button nose in the middle. Going back was a mask of black with large, expressive, dark brown eyes. In the very center of his black head was a substantial white tuft of hair. His paws looked big and flat, not pointed and slim like a Poodle's. The white areas showed black intermittent spots almost Dalmatian like.

"Sam wants a female Poodle and you definitely aren't one of those, but I'll see what I can do," I explain to the dog. I feel that he will understand the tone and that I was trying to communicate something, always preferable to being ignored. Whether or not he's fully grown I have no idea. I only know that I have great difficulty prying myself from his cage. Walking away, I turn back, and see defeat written all over his despondent black and white face. "I will be back," I call. Not actually sure about that, I know deep down that I want this dog. Driving home I still feel those eyes on me. But what about Sam? I wonder if I could talk him into two dogs. Maybe there was a slim chance. The Poodle is a given. I'd promised. I call later that day to tell Nancy that Sam was about to drive over to see the Poodle.

After a slight pause, she says "I'm sorry. The Poodle's gone." I'm taken aback.

"What do you mean?! I told you I thought we'd take her."

"Yes, but one of the volunteers noticed on her chart that she'd bitten a man. I don't want to have any problems, so I gave her to two women." I don't believe what I'm hearing. "But the black and white Poodle mix is still available," Nancy says encouragingly. I hang up and tell Sam the news.

"At least we know that the Poodle got a permanent home." Sam agreed to drive over and look at the fellow in the cage. I feel certain that the dog contains not even one percent Poodle. His unusual looks, with that penetrating gaze were quite arresting, but the thick paws resembled those of a small Sheepdog with the same irregular black and white coloring many of them have. But, hey, I wanted this dog and figure I could just quote the rescue lady, right? Sam would see what he was or wasn't for himself.

About an hour and a half later Sam returns, decidedly unenthusiastic.

"What'd you think" I ask him.

"I don't know," he shrugs. "He's funny looking." Yeah, for a Poodle, I say to myself. "Big head, skinny body. He didn't pay any attention to me when I took him for a walk."

"Of course not. You're probably just one of many who come by and let him out."

"If you want him, it's o.k. He doesn't look much like a Poodle." I couldn't argue with that. Sam's usual good nature still intact, he was no longer terribly interested in the whole dog thing. Have I ruined this whole adoption thing which was supposed to be a mutual project? What kind of wife am I? I want him to be enthusiastic, excited, and recognize the something special I've seen in the dog. Should I keep searching for a Poodle? I mull it over. What if we got the dog and Sam never likes him much?

The next day, Nancy, who runs Perfect Pet Rescue, is at her weekly post, a street corner in Santa Monica where my unhappy, little friend and a half dozen of his similarly situated cohorts sat on display with kerchiefs on their necks, hoping to be chosen for adoption. Nancy goes to the pound every week and picks up a half dozen dogs she thinks are adoptable, takes them to the hospital to get whatever care they need, then tries to find them homes. What strength that takes. If I did that I'd dissolve over the ones getting left behind.

"I have a strong feeling that dog will be adopted today," I tell Sam in the middle of our tennis game. I rationalize that Sam isn't set against this guy. We leave to again see Chester, the dog's temporary name.

Sounds English but doesn't fit him. He seems docile when we walk him. A quiet dog, definitely a mutt, neither too big nor too small.

"You know mutts have better health," I proclaim, my opening statement to the jury. "No inbreeding." Sam nods, still obviously less than keen on the little fellow than I am. "So many of the pedigrees are bred for looks rather than health or performance." Over a sandwich at the market next door, we discuss Chester. "We can still look for a Poodle to keep this one company," I suggest. But the jury revealed nothing.

"He's thought to be between one and a half and two," Nancy has told us. "I know nothing else about him except he was in the worse shelter in the City. Before that he was picked up on the streets."

I want so much for Sam to be crazy about this dog, but he just isn't. Nonetheless, good natured to his core, he wants me to make the decision. What if things never got any better between Sam and the dog? What if he turns out to be a horror who rips up the new house we just built? My gut, however, tells me that the little guy might be the right match for us, two middle age people who didn't need any messy housebreaking or house wrecking challenges. At one and a half to two he was probably trained, a definite plus. But getting a dog is a lifetime commitment. His lifetime will be our responsibility, even if we leave this earth before him. We had to make plans.

I'm a small time gambler. "We'll take him," we finally tell Nancy. Our canine parenthood was about to begin. And like all parenthood, it wasn't exactly as planned.

Chapter 2

FOR BETTER OR WORSE?

We give dogs time we can spare, space we can spare and love we can spare. And in return, dogs give us their all. It's the best deal man has ever made.

M. ACKLAM

After filling out an application, answering a few questions and paying an adoption fee, we tell Nancy "we'll go buy all the supplies and pick him up tomorrow."

"Really? Are you going to make him sleep in a cage one more night?" she asks reprovingly. Clearly Nancy knows about Jewish guilt. That's all we need to hear. The three of us leave, with leash, collar, vaccination certificates, drops for an ear infection and antibiotics for a kennel cough. "The worms he has will soon be gone," Nancy assures us. Sam shoots me a skeptical look. Worms?! She'd never mentioned those before. Or the ears or the cough. So much for healthy mutts, but we're still saving a homeless dog.

"I'll come by tomorrow to show you how to put in his eardrops," Nancy promises. "His neutering is included in the fee and can be done at the hospital where he's been boarded." We notice that he has only one testicle. I wonder if that entitles us to a fifty percent discount on such a procedure. I'm not asking.

We decide to call our adoptee Chips, after the brown mutt who'd been the brief joy of my childhood. I met his namesake, a special dog to me, when I was ten or twelve. The most pedestrian of brown mutts, Chips seemed a paragon of canine beauty, who shortly wound himself around my heart. His "owners," a kindly couple whose children were grown and gone, lived across the street from my family. After school, I'd walk and play with the dog. Several times, the woman, Mrs. Goldberg, was late getting home, but that never stopped Chips and I from "conversing" through the door. Whether he howled, barked or moaned, I answered in kind. This practice amused me and, whatever we talked about, seemed to engage Chips. I was soon given a key to the Goldbergs' house.

A few years of Chips' and my mutual love and deepening relationship sped by.

Eventually, the Goldbergs moved away, taking Chips with them, I hope. Only many years later did I learn that they first offered him to my parents, who had refused without telling me. Their rationale – Chips was an older dog who would probably die in a few years, which would hurt me. Instead I was hurt a lot sooner. I missed my friend every day after that. Now I had a chance to do right by another dog.

I'm surprised that Chips II doesn't know how to get into our car and seems completely unfamiliar with riding in one. He doesn't quite know where to go, so I pick him up and hold him on my lap as we head to the pet store. He feels like about twenty pounds of dog, at least ten of those being profound timidity. An hour later we leave the store with $156 worth of supplies, including a seatbelt, which I've read that dogs need for safe car rides.

At home, when we pet Chips, he lowers his head before adjusting to a normal position. Clearly he's been abused. An approaching hand frightens him. Figuring that being on his level would frighten him less, we begin crouching down first before petting him. It seems to help….him. But I get stuck down there the first few times and need a hand up. After a little practice I can actually return to an upright position myself. Maybe the dog would get me into better shape or I'd spend the rest of my life on the floor.

Until Chips' toilet skills can be ascertained we decide to close him into the kitchen, laundry and small exercise room area while we're out of the house. The back room, with nylon washable carpet, is dog safe. The kitchen and laundry area have easy to clean stone floors. This house and all its furniture are new. We don't want to chance disaster when we go out. But just to be safe, I'd bought the floor cleaner to remove any pet accidents that might occur.

The first day home Chips seems housebroken, knows what to do on walks, coughs, and sleeps a lot. He never barks. More reluctant than exuberant, the dog won't venture into our back yard without us. Whenever we go up the stairs to our bedroom or Sam's office, he stands at the bottom of the staircase and whimpers. We assume he's never seen stairs before, or wasn't allowed where they led. Not only did he come from a shelter but a sheltered life for sure.

On the first day with us we give Chips a rawhide stick to chew on. He grabs it like a baby with a pacifier, and won't let go. After a few minutes I see blood coming out of his mouth and notice that he's already chipped a bottom front tooth on the rawhide. Sam stares at me accusingly, as if I'd given the dog arsenic. "Take if away from him," he says. I try to take the rawhide away to better inspect the tooth. A soft growl follows. You aint gettin' my treat back, he seems to say. Shocked, we both back off.

"This may be the only treat he's ever had," I tell Sam, deciding not to correct the behavior. Subconsciously I must have decided to have Sam associate the day Chips came to live with us with a great meal; I begin fixing his favorite dinner, coq au vin. Thus, I feel justified asking him to take Chips for a walk so I can get it going.

"All right. He'll probably let go of the rawhide."

"Sure, if he's busy sniffing and peeing." A half hour later, Sam returns with Chips still possessively grasping that rawhide in his teeth.

"Amazing! He went for a half hour's walk without dropping it once." We let him be. He keeps the rawhide with him until we go to sleep. On that first night, still considering potential potty accidents, we don't encourage him to follow us upstairs. Instead, we close him into the same three back rooms, where he cries and whimpers.

"How lonely Chips must be" I tell Sam. He nods. We're both hanging out in the hallway upstairs, sleepless while we worry about the dog. We think about bringing him upstairs, but then look at the new bedroom rug. He stays down. Naturally, guilt makes sleep troubled and brief. Round one – three losers; no winners.

The next day, when we go into the backyard, our new resident ducks under a bush where he thinks he's unobserved, and buries the rawhide. That's the last time we ever see it. As Chips' background's completely unknown it has to be deduced from his personality and actions. We deduce abuse and neglect. He still lowers his head when approached, is hesitant about trying anything new, and unduly concerned by all that we do. No doubt his skinniness points to a lack of food, either on the streets or in his former home. I intend to fix that right away.

On top of Chips' other maladies, he skips with his back right leg about a quarter of the time he walks. "Either he was kicked or injured some other way" Sam tells me, conjuring up the Dickensian puppyhood to which the dog must have been subjected. The next day we visit a recommended, nearby vet. He can find nothing wrong with Chips' hind leg, but his skipping continues intermittently. In time he lifts it up less and less. But the problem remains for a few years.

That first morning with Chips, Nancy arrives as promised to demonstrate how to put in the eardrops for Chips' infection.

"Just flip up the ear, and quickly squeeze in a few drops of ointment." That looks do-able to me.

"His history of hunger is obvious" I say. "Every time I begin to prepare his chow, he stands on his hind legs, with his paws up against the counter, frantic, panting to get to it. After 'inhaling' it in two seconds flat, he throws up."

"The overcrowding at the pound, like most shelters, forced him into a cage with two big dogs who apparently didn't let him near the food." Nancy gleaned this from the shelter people. Chips had only gotten regular nourishment for the few days he was in the veterinary hospital.

"Try elevating the food. Some dogs don't do well eating with their heads down." "O.K." I grab two large phone books and stick them under Chips' plate. Sure enough, it works perfectly. And the L.A. phonebooks are finally getting some good use. Unlike the few directories in New York, there are so many phonebooks in Los Angeles for different areas that most people give up finding phone numbers anywhere but on the internet. Occasionally, the food dishes slide off the books, so we eventually get one of those small wooden stands with legs and two dishes in it. Sam dubs it Chips' "dining room table."

On our second night with our new dog, still unable to sleep, we're in the hallway listening to his whimpers and cries. "It's just awful," Sam says, maybe slightly less indifferent to the dog than he was before.

"Should we let him up?"

"Are you sure he's housebroken?"

"I can't give you a written guarantee." We both glance at the new rug.

"Maybe we wait another night."

"I'm exhausted." Thus convincing ourselves that this is still the right thing to do, we spend another sleepless eight hours trying not to hear Chips. By the third night, concluding that he appears to be house-broken, we call him upstairs at bedtime. He puts one tentative paw on the first step and tries it out. This is followed by whimpers. "Come on pup" I call. Finally, with much coaxing from us, he catches on, placing one paw slowly after another, eventually reaching the landing and coming into our bedroom. There, he stares longingly at a beige club chair, but doesn't jump on it.

"Wow! He was really trained, probably too harshly." I cover the chair with a towel, after which I gesture to Chips to climb aboard. He jumps right up. I have never seen a dog who actually waited to be invited like that. Round two – three winners, no losers. We all get some desperately needed rest. Chips ailments, however, remain with us. Would he ever get better?

Chapter 3

A DOG BY ANY OTHER NAME

"If dogs are not there, it is not heaven."

ELIZABETH MARSHALL THOMAS

"Maybe you should take him to the vet," Sam mumbles a week later from behind his Wall Street Journal. "That cough isn't getting better." The vet visit I know will eat into my already shrinking work time, but if the guy is sick....I take Chips to the doctor and have his antibiotic changed. In the vet's waiting room, a chaotic arena of nervous, whining, shifting dogs under guardians' legs, on laps, in front of seats, Chips sees an aggressive four pounder showing her teeth and growling at another dog. Suddenly, my silent boy barks his head off. He could speak! It's the first time I've heard him sound like a real dog.

We are finally called in.

"Looks like a Tibetan Terrier, probably a pure-breed," the vet announces.

"What?! I thought he was a mutt." I've never heard of a Tibetan Terrier at this point. They're not as popular as they're shortly to become. Next the doctor examines Chips' teeth.

"Seems about two years old." Immediately after leaving, I drive to the library, take a book on dog breeds off the shelf, look up "Tibetan Terrier," and there is Chips!...albeit with a lot less hair than the ones in the book. Back in my car I show Chips, now in the front passenger seat, the picture. He seems unimpressed. The irony! I'm someone who actually preferred a mutt and ended up with a fancy, fairly rare dog from a rescue group, which labeled him a Poodle mix. According to the photos in the book, Chips appears the perfect, if thin, specimen with the characteristic curved tail of the Tibetan. Though his dull, rough coat is shaved down to a crew cut, the pictures show long, luxurious double coats.

Born in several colors and color combinations, these dogs, the book indicates, were never bred for a particular one. They were raised by monks in Tibetan monasteries for two thousand years and are highly prized as companions and bringers of good luck. I just knew our guy had an important job to do. Traditionally they were given as gifts, but never sold in Tibet, as it was thought that one would be selling part of one's luck. God knows I can't afford to let go of any of that in my profession.

The article further states that these dogs are not genuine Terriers or working dogs, but only called that because of their size and build. In the "non-sporting" class, they were first brought to the United States in 1956, having grown in popularity. Now they are coveted for their sensitivity, intelligence, happy nature and loyalty. Indeed, Chips' improving mood was beginning to show in his frequently wagging tail. I could vouch for the "non-sporting" bit as Chips was showing himself to be a devoted couch potato.

"He's actually a Tibetan Terrier," I inform Sam, thinking Chips' new identity will elevate him in my husband's estimation. This news does not seem to be the thrill for Sam that I expect. And Chips, unaware of his honorable ancestry, finds nothing humiliating in lying outside the bathroom door whenever I go inside, crying if I take longer than he deems necessary. I actually hear him putting his snout to the bottom of the door and sniffing while I'm in there. Yes, sniffing like some wine critics. Well, to each his own vintage.

"Velcro" Sam dubs him, as he watches the dog trail after me from room to room. Gradually our boy begins barking when anyone comes near our door, with an uncharacteristically loud voice for his size. Eventually Chips barks whenever anyone passes even close to the house. This inevitably happens whenever Sam is on an important business call. "Shhh," I tell Chips, holding his snout a moment, while the delivery person shows up or some gardener or pool man passes too close to our property for Chips' comfort. Though Sam's professional status is not enhanced by this racket, Chips proves incapable of suppressing his emotions and instincts at such times. I leap into action if Sam is on a call, but usually only succeed in reducing Chips' bark to more of a whine which I hope cannot be as readily heard in Sam's office on the second floor. When not barking, Chips keeps his vocalizing to a kind of cry or whine, which he does for all sorts of reasons other than anxiety.

Happily for me, Sam begins, as the days roll by, to increasingly get a kick out of each new thing that Chips does. I am hoping that in time the dog's non-Poodleness will be a moot point.

"He's your dog," Sam announces one morning. "Just so you know, I'm not going to feed or walk him." What could I say? Chips was really my choice, but Sam's disappointing proclamation puts him clearly on a separate team from me and Chips. However, one day when I have a meeting at a network my reluctant husband really has no choice. Annoyed but resigned, he picks up the plastic poop bags and trudges out. When I come home I find him, surprisingly, much cheerier.

"I sure wish I'd known about this when I was single," he announces smiling. "Women are wildly attracted to this little guy – a blonde in an old T-bird actually stopped driving to discuss him. One brunette reversed her direction and bent down to coo over him!"

"Maternal instinct no doubt."

"You mean I get no credit for this myself?"

"I'm sure the guy walking him had everything to do with it," I assure him.

"And then two college coeds crossed the street just to meet him!" Sam had found himself in discussions about and 'petting sessions' with Chips and a variety of attractive female admirers. Most women naturally like dogs, but Chips seems a magnet for them, probably because he appears like nothing so much as an over-sized stuffed toy come to life. A youthful, affectionate personality combined with a sweet, expressive face and a habit of always making eye contact renders him irresistible to women. Our dog's finer points have suddenly become apparent to my husband. Actually expecting him to help me on a continuing basis, though, proves too much at this point.

As Chips gains weight and gets over his initial maladies his curved tail starts wagging continuously and his usual friendliness increases tenfold. Most dog parents discover that there's nothing as easy as meeting people when walking an inviting canine. Both species are social animals. Some dogs just attract women more than men. Though I must say that with Chips we met plenty of both. This social phenomenon is a wonderful boon for shy people. Making friends over a four legged companion seems to be the easiest thing in the world. Dogs break down all the normal social barriers by immediately establishing a common point of reference.

"Do you have an extra poop bag?" or "Who's your groomer?" Of course if the other person has no dog, these questions may get you a few strange looks, but asking about someone's dog is considered appreciative, never nosey. Talking about one's own past or present dog resembles the human baby connection. Those who have them like to talk to about them, especially with others who do too.

After he's been with us a few weeks, I start taking him with me on errands. "Isn't he the dearest thing" a young woman at Saks' Clinique makeup counter says to me while coming around to pet Chips. In two minutes flat, he has a bevy of beautiful young women petting and fussing over him from all the surrounding makeup counters. "How old is he" another asks.

"I think about two years." A guy nearby witnessing this encounter, walks over. "Can I borrow him for a while? I just got divorced."

"An excellent strategy" I tell him, "but his time goes for a high fee."

By now we've settled into a routine. When Chips wakes up, he comes over and stands on his hind legs on my side of the bed, the better to see if I'm awake. He will not jump on the bed or try to wake me. But this little peek in the morning is irresistible. I get up and take him for a mile or two walk, then return for breakfast. On the street where we usually go, Jay Leno often drives by in one of his many sports cars; he always waves, not because I know him, which I don't, but just because I think he recognizes Chips and is as friendly off the small screen as on.

I quickly discover on these walks that Chips has no love of rap music. If someone listening to it passes in his car, Chips barks aggressively at him. No fan of rap music myself, I confess to not discouraging him. Does anyone else think it's ironic that when someone in a car plays rap music, he always keeps the windows open? Even if it's ninety degrees? Perhaps trying to annoy others is a greater pleasure than listening to this music. Chips makes clear his musical preferences at home too. If I sit down to play the piano, struggling with my classical and old time popular pieces, he always moves close. Seems his musical tastes are consistent with ours. A couple of times he actually jumps on the piano bench.

Another strange thing – our four legged charge pays a lot of attention to pickup trucks and wants to walk into construction sites. Could he have belonged to one of those construction guys who keep their dogs in the back of trucks? It's difficult to imagine Mr. Sensitivity nestled among tools or gardening supplies on the hard surface of a truck.

Sam, Chips and I now eat together, in the sense of the same time. Chips has not yet graduated to our kitchen table, though in time, who knows what he expects? If we put Chips' food down and leave the room, he immediately stops eating.

"Don't you like it" I ask the first time he follows me out of the kitchen. He leads me back to the food and begins eating again. No matter how succulent the morsels, nothing will keep Chips chomping away if he's alone in the room. When we go out for dinner, I feed him first but have to remain in the kitchen until he finishes his chow. How much more sociable could a fellow be than putting companionship above food? No wonder people love their dogs.

I notice that Chips does a lot of cat-like self cleaning, licking himself wherever he can reach. And always taking a keen interest in anything Chips focuses on, we notice one day, during his licking routine, that the hair around his genitalia appears slightly orange.

"Maybe he's got blood in his urine," Sam suggests, "which means possible prostate cancer. If we're lucky it's only a urine infection. You should take in a sample, maybe two, to the vet." I could not believe Mr. Doom and Gloom's melodramatic scenario. Still, if there's a possibility that something is wrong... but I know the vet is likely to take me less seriously if I walk in for the third time in ten days. Sam's tone becomes increasingly dire. "And if it is prostate cancer, he will probably have to wear diapers. Are you going to put him down if he has to wear diapers?!" he asks reprovingly.

"No. I'll hire a full time nurse." I've heard the definite personal note in his question but decide to wait a day or two before taking Chips in again. Sure enough, the discoloration disappears.

In the meantime, I can't avoid another vet visit because the ear scratching has returned. Despite using the eardrops, nothing has improved. And his tolerance for us putting them in has hit zero. Chips moves his strong head all around whenever either of us approaches with the ear dropper. The vet gives us new drops but their administration becomes a two parent job, one of us holding his head while the other flips up the ear and puts in the drops. Despite Sam's trying to distance himself from getting too involved with our boy, he participates in these medical treatments because he sees that they're impossible without his help.

And another health concern emerges – Chips constantly chews and licks his paws, which grow redder. I call Nancy. "They might be irritated from the ammonia mixture used to wash down the shelter cage floors. It's very harsh, but they need to keep them clean." Now Sam and I feel even sorrier for this poor guy than we did before. After another week the paw licking and chewing do not improve. We vow to do something about it.

Chapter 4

ONLY IN L. A.

Scratch a dog and you'll find a permanent job.

FRANKLIN P. JONES

We take Chips to a department store to let him look around and see what he needs. Actually, socializing him as soon as possible seems like a good idea. If he's never been up stairs, he's probably been very few places. An outing to a new place might distract him from his ailments and scratching. We strap him into his new seatbelt, which really requires the dog to sit up facing forward to work properly. But Chips lies down, twists around and eventually gets so tangled in the straps that he can't move.

At the store, we need to go to the second floor. Escalators are clearly out of the question. A mangled paw would not be useful right now. So we enter the large elevator. Chips requires even more coaxing than with the stairs to get in, but when this "room" with a movable door begins rising, he freaks out, shifting side to side, making anxious crying noises. We pet him, saying "It's o.k. It's good." When the door opens he bolts out, pulling the leash right from my hand. After chasing him through dishes and bedding, I finally get him back in control and head for the towel department.

While we talk towels with a salesman, a woman nearby begins laughing. I turn to see her watching Chips, now staring at himself in the long mirror on the floor. He walks toward the dog in the reflection, touches the glass with his paw, then explores the back of the mirror. After doing this a few times, he just stares at the dog in the glass and whines. Whatever he concludes about the "other guy" he never again tries to analyze a mirror. Pretty clever, I think. Only one try and he gets it, or at least realizes there is no getting it. Maybe he's got advanced training possibilities.

When we're done with our shopping, we reverse the elevator process. Chips needs a lot more convincing to get in this contraption the second time. "Come on Chips." He won't budge. It's a question of dragging him by the neck or trying reverse psychology. I opt for the latter, letting go of the leash and letting it drop, making believe I'm going without him. That does it. He decides that braving this thing is a better alternative than being left behind. After that first store visit, Chips sometimes catches his reflection in a mirror at our house, pauses and looks at it briefly, but now seems nonchalant about the whole technology.

A few months after getting Chips, another shopping excursion takes place. I need a new car and decide on a Saab. The three of us go to the dealer to see if Chips can manage to jump into the back seat. I don't want to have to lift his now twenty-five pounds each time we use the car, so if he finds it too high, the Saab is out. While examining the sedan I open the back door; Chips has no problem jumping in. After taking a test drive we come back to the car lot. There, another couple with a family pet also weighs the pros and cons of purchasing a Saab......only their pet is a pig. That's right – about 250 pounds worth.

The couple has brought the family pig, obviously some kind of smaller breed, to see if she can get into the car. Their pride and joy, kind of a charcoal grey, stands placidly in her harness and leash. Very curious about this creature, Chips slowly, carefully approaches, sniffing the air. The animal stands on four legs and has a tail, but apparently does not smell like a dog. Our boy stops about five feet away. Something tells him she might not welcome his advances. I also wouldn't let him get any closer. The husband and wife who own this pig walk around a station wagon type car with a back that opens fairly low to the ground. Nonetheless, they have a ramp with them to make sure the pig with her short legs can climb up into the car. The question seems to be, "Would she?"

"If she won't get in, we can't take it" the man says definitively to the salesman. The salesman opens the very back door of the station wagon and waits anxiously for the pig to enter, while the couple places their pet's ramp against the car. We all watch with trepidation. The pig stares at the ramp, stands at the bottom, but doesn't move. The "owners" cluck and encourage all they can, with the salesman joining in. Everyone stands around pulling for the pig to climb up that ramp, but the heavyset girl stands her ground. Such are the vagaries of car sales in Los Angeles. Things look grim for a sales transaction when Chips, who apparently grasps the gist of everyone's desire suddenly jumps into the back seat of that car, which also has an open rear passenger door. I'm about to order him out when he starts barking right at the pig.

Sam and I laugh because there's no doubt but that Chips has joined in trying to get the animal up that ramp. Though the two species could not have spoken the same language, soon the pig puts one hoof on the ramp. I'm flabbergasted. Everyone starts praising her while Chips keeps up his barking. His tail wags faster as the hefty girl tentatively places one hoof after another, eventually making her way up that ramp. When she reaches the open back of the car, Chips decides that his job's done. He jumps out and the pig gets in. Maybe he just wants to distance himself from her. I think that the salesman will kiss Chips, but he only gets a pat on the head and a promise of "cookies next time." The other couple does buy the station wagon and we buy the sedan. All in all, a terrific day for the salesman. Whenever he sees Chips after that, you can bet he has some dog treats on hand. I let him know Chips' preference would be chicken or steak.

Back at home, I pop out of bed ahead of my husband each day to take our boy for a walk. Mornings, Sam's and my former preferred times for romantic encounters, are filled with the care and feeding of Chips. I fear this will do nothing to endear him to Sam. Would my husband end up resenting me for putting Chips' needs first? I hoped my gamble wouldn't throw a wrench into our otherwise smooth running marriage. But a more dire problem emerges.

Chapter 5

SEPARATION ANXIETY

Outside of a dog, a book is man's best friend.
Inside a dog, it's too dark to read.

GROUCHO MARX

Whenever we get ready to leave the house without him, Chips throws himself into a let-it-all-hang-out, submissive position on his back. That failing to hold us, he crawls to the door and grabs one of our feet with his paws. "Don't leave me! Please don't leave me" I almost hear him cry. My guilt grows every time I go, but life outside of Chips' domain needs to be lived – groceries need to be bought, doctors need to be visited and so on. After eventually detaching his paws from our ankles, we open the door, trying to squeeze out of the partially opened barrier. But heartbreaking crying and maneuvers to block us continue whenever we leave the house. Naturally, Chips tries to bolt out ahead of us; once he succeeds.

"Oh no!" I yell. On our corner, where three streets meet, there's often traffic coming from up the hill, down the hill or around the bend. We have a fence and a gate, but the gate just happens to be open for some delivery guy at the moment our dog runs out. Chips charges up the hill around the corner with Sam and me in frantic pursuit, both our hearts midway to our throats. We know that the most common way dogs die is getting run over – my mother's dog was one of them. Traffic here moves fast. We don't want to be two more pet parents who can't figure out how to protect their dog. By now we're panting away as the hill keeps going up and up, and Chips with it. Traffic here is not heavy but cars move too fast to easily avoid a dog. I'm terrified and keep screaming "Chips!"

A gardener up the hill sees us running after the dog. He manages to grab Chips by his collar when he stops to sniff. "Muchisimas gracias por salvar mi per-rito," Sam, originally from Cuba, gasps in his native tongue as we reach the man.

"De nada." The men shake hands.

"Don't put us through that again, o.k.?" I tell Chips. "We'd never survive the guilt trip if you got run over." I walk home carrying him. Lucky to get him back this once, we vow never to let it happen again.

After two weeks with no accidents or chewing on furniture, Chips' inspires enough confidence in us so that the next time we leave, we don't lock him in the kitchen and back room, but let him have the run of the house. Perhaps his separation anxiety will go away if he actually sees us walk out the front door.

Gone a mere two hours, we return and find no damage...or so we think. Evidently Chips has been on the living room couch. One pillow is down. O.K. He probably went there to look out the window. Climbing on the furniture doesn't concern us, especially as he's a `non-shedding breed. But on further inspection, we see a small rip with teeth marks – and they aren't ours – in the drapes. I gave up drape chewing years ago.

"He obviously tried to open it. It's our fault," I announce hoping that Sam wouldn't be upset. "We should have left the drape open so that he could see where we went."

"Right." Sam to my amazement agrees. "Anyway, a man on a galloping horse won't notice that little tear." I'm relieved that he takes this so well. Is Sam becoming fonder of Chips than he intended? Our boy listens intently to this discussion, wagging his tail, probably realizing that whatever he did must have been all right.

From that point on, Chips goes wherever he wants, though I do place towels over the light or delicate furniture. Changed on a weekly basis, the towels remain for the rest of Chips' life. So much for interior decorating and deliberations over color scheme. The next time we leave the house, we see Chips watching out the same living room window. When we return, all looks fine. "Hey come here," Sam calls from the dining room. "Look what he's done." There he shows me scratches on the bottom half of the ceiling to floor windows – right into the coating that we had installed to protect them. God knows what that will cost to correct. Or maybe we shouldn't bother to fix them, given that Chips still has his nails and anxiety. His canine brain probably assumes that there's some way to open the darn things if he keeps at them. The run of the house isn't working as we'd imagined.

Back to the kitchen for Chips. But we hate confining him, so the next day I decide to try to solve his separation anxiety at the root of the problem. My friend knows a pet store owner who's an expert on behavioral problems. I drive over there.

"Put the dog in a cage and cover it with a sheet," the man tells me. "When he cries, bang on the top of it. He'll think it's an earthquake and associate it with crying. Soon the crying will stop." Of course. He'll be too busy talking to his shrink about his repressed emotions and fear of earthquakes. I hastily leave this guy's store with a "thank you." We do not buy a cage.

As Chips' separation anxiety grows, so does my guilt over leaving him for our numerous excursions to movies, theatre, my Writers Guild committee meetings, concerts, visits with friends and family. I weigh my options. I could stay home and give up the rest of my life. This idea isn't instantly dismissed. One evening, we decide to let the video camera run while we're out so that we could see just how bad this problem really gets. Hopefully, after we're gone a while, Chips settles down and goes to sleep.

When we return and view the video, it's filled with two hours of heartbreaking crying and howling accompanied by Chips wandering around or sitting down. This does nothing to assuage our guilt. The howling resembles a real wolf-like cry of despair and loneliness, according to the behaviorists whose books I've read.

"Maybe we should just stay home all the time," Sam, reading my mind, says. Something tells me he's only half kidding. There seems to be no easy answers for Chips' emotional problem. I briefly consider doggy Prozac which might help some, but feel he's too young to start on drugs like that. After all, what kind of mother was I if the only solution to my ward's emotional problems was to put him on mind altering drugs. On the other hand, if I didn't solve the problem it was me who would end up taking drugs. I had to weigh all the alternatives.

"Should we get another dog to keep him company," I wonder aloud.

But our friends who have two dogs tell us they're less interested in each other than they are in their humans. "Unless they were litter mates or were gotten together, they often don't play together, and sometimes compete for attention," one couple says. Also, Tibetans, according to the literature, are extremely people oriented and consider themselves one of us. When they can't go along, they're miserable. This point is apparently lost on the local authorities who insist on keeping dogs out of the Farmer's Market, an outdoor arena, restaurants and museums.

Chips relates to other dogs well but briefly, then returns his focus to us. Rather than put him into a deeper depression when we leave, we begin taking him everywhere we can. If we had two dogs, it would be difficult to even fit them both under an outdoor restaurant table. Chips quickly learns that "come back soon," means we're leaving without him. "Chips is going" soon become his three very favorite words, eliciting mad tail wagging and euphoric body language. We're surprised at how fast Chips picks up vocabulary.

"I've read that dogs can retain about two hundred words," Sam tells me. After a while, "we come back soon," a euphemism for "you're not coming," initiates the slowdown of his tail until it stops moving altogether. He then usually heads for the small space between the living room couch and the end table, a place we dub "the hole," to pout. We hate being the bearer of bad tidings, but the world unfortunately does not welcome dogs in many places we have to go.

One Sunday, I get up at seven to call "The Pet Show" on the radio and ask Warren Eckstein, my favorite animal behaviorist, how to resolve the separation anxiety. I get a busy signal, but keep redialing like crazy. Finally I get through. The screener puts me on hold for twenty-five minutes while I listen to commercials and the show. He comes back and asks my problem.

When I try to explain that Chips cannot handle any separation from us he says, "We have an almost identical call. If your question isn't answered, call next Saturday at 6." Boom. I'm disconnected. The call he referred to is about a woman who leaves her dog all day while she works, then comes home for five minutes and goes back out shopping. Her dog is upset when she leaves the second time. Are you serious?! That dog is alone all day. Then he's expected to be happy about being left again! She should be brought up on abuse charges. My dog is with me all day, except when I'm in the bathroom. And he can barely handle *that*.

"I know a terrific trainer" another dog loving friend tells us. "She'll know exactly how to handle this problem."

Michelle, the trainer, arrives and immediately warns us "If you don't solve this separation anxiety, Chips might hurl himself through a plate glass window to get to you after you leave". Oh, great; now we're potential murderers. "Dogs have died from this," she insists. That does a lot to make us feel better. I have visions of a blood soaked dog having barely survived a leap through our dining room windows, charging around the neighborhood until he's picked up by the authorities.

"O.K. we want to fix the problem." First, Michelle puts Chips on a leash and ties him to the piano leg across the living room. When he cries and strains at the leash to get to us, Michelle stamps her foot and tells him to be quiet. Startled, he stops crying. Michelle then throws him a small cookie for a reward. I gasp. After several repetitions, we all leave the room. Chips' howling grows desperate. Sam and I begin to hyper-ventilate.

"What is the point of this?" Sam demands.

"To make him control his crying. After a while, you'll be able to leave him for longer and longer with no crying or acting out." But the crying isn't the problem; his anxiety is. Michelle leaves.

"It would be much easier to tie ourselves to the piano leg," I say, "rather than watch him go through such desperation again." Sam agrees, reacting as I did. Finally, we forge our own solution – take Chips with us whenever possible, even if it means leaving him in the car alone for a short time. This we usually do on a well travelled street with pedestrians and stores so that there's something for him to watch. If it's too hot to keep him in the car and we must leave him at home, we assure him of our imminent return, putting the TV on either the cartoon channel or PBS.

Sam tells me, "I've read that dogs have the intel-lectual capacity of an 18 month old child." Though it depends on whose child one is discussing, we decide that the cartoon channel would suit Chips if he's on grade level or, if he's gifted, PBS would work nicely. Animal Planet is out. It contains some violent material about rescuing abused animals in the evenings that might upset him. National Geographic, the Cartoon Channel or PBS soon become our stations of choice.

Chips now has the run of the house. Though no more damage ever ensues to our far less important material possessions, we are not out of the woods.

The stress and worry around Chips' emotional state becomes part of Sam's and my psychological undercurrent as we go increasingly bonkers over our black and white boy. No doubt, he is now ours and we are now his.

A few weeks after Chips comes to live with us, Sam needs to go to San Francisco for a short meeting and doctor's appointment. I promised to go with him. "Aunt Berta," Sam's older sister, never a dog lover, none-theless volunteers to babysit. We're concerned about leaving Chips with someone new, but feel that Berta, a sweet, loving woman, will do her level best. And Chips would learn some Spanish, as my sister-in-law still feels more comfortable in her native tongue. She was the last arrival in her family to emigrate from Cuba.

Berta receives more instructions on how to care for our canine than do most nurses for a newborn human. "When Chips cries, just try baby talk," I suggest. "Lots of petting goes without saying." She gives us a dubious nod as we leave. Sam calls from the airport to see if the dog has survived our departure. Apparently, he's still breathing, and has eaten breakfast, but hasn't done his "business" on his first walk with the dog walker we hired. Berta's bad back and our location in the hills make it impossible for her to walk the Chips herself. By the time of Sam's second call, placed in the afternoon, Chips still hadn't pooped, but the occasional whimpers we'd come to know as loneliness or anxiety were now subsiding, we were told.

After Sam's appointment, we enter a beautiful restaurant where we have a reservation for dinner. On several previous trips to San Francisco we'd been unable to get into this popular, highly regarded place. We sit down at the candlelit table. Sam orders two glasses of wine and we starts looking over the menu. He read my thoughts.

"Chips probably thinks we're gone for good. We've never left him this long." Exactly. I looked in admiration at my husband. Obviously, we're both worried that Chips feels abandoned by us. The dog's separation anxiety had turned into ours. While we began talking about the food, Sam closes his menu. "What's one more fancy dinner?"

I smile at him. Lucky for me, he had become as crazy about Chips as I was. We both get up. Heading for the airport early to catch the next flight, we call home again. Sam questioned Berta on the elimination situation and discovers that Chips has pooped aplenty in our yard. He simply went to the door when he had to go and, sure enough, there was a human to open it. All was well. My husband seems blissfully unaware that his sister now questions his mental health.

I expect smooth sailing for the foreseeable future, but I guess I'd never navigated with a dog like Chips.

Chapter 6

TOUGH LOVE, TOUGH CHOICES

---

*For it is by muteness that a dog becomes for one
so utterly beyond value; with him one is at peace,
where words play no torturing tricks.*

JOHN GALSWORTHY

In a matter of months, I notice that the stimulating
banter Sam and I normally enjoyed over breakfast and
our newspaper has given way to profound questions
like, "Why doesn't Chips play with any of his toys?"
"How's his stool?" and "Why doesn't he want to chase
balls, play frisbee, anything?" The breaking news of
the day, the latest play or political scandal takes a back
seat to these vital issues. There's no doubt anymore
that Chips has exploded our universe – exploded and

expanded. We are now his parents, caretakers, owners, guardians – whatever term you like. But without a doubt, he is ours and we are his. Still, Sam remains partially ambivalent.

One morning my "shadow," Sam's alternate moniker for him, suddenly disappears from my sight, a rare occurrence. Very suspicious. I walk into the kitchen to check, and find Chips sitting in the middle of a pile of garbage which he's gotten into by making a hole in the garbage bag Sam had unwittingly left on the kitchen floor. His tail thumps happily.

"What did you do?" I ask, as if it isn't perfectly obvious. Day old raw chicken parts, orange peels, left over salad surround my boy. Coffee grounds cover his mouth and he's eating something. I know that whatever it is will probably make him sick. I actually say "bad boy," for the first and last time in our relationship, while fishing some vegetable peels out of his mouth. I immediately realize that label belongs to his daddy for leaving the garbage in a bag there.

Chips puts his head down, looking defeated. Consumed with regret for scolding him, and knowing that he's too timid anyway, I remind myself that what Chips needs is praise to build the confidence he clearly lacks. I vow never to use the B word in his presence again.

Expunging it from our vocabulary, whenever Sam and I need to use it again to each other, we spell. This becomes such an ingrained habit that a few times we find ourselves spelling "bad" when we're alone, and laugh at our foolishness. On those rare occasions that Chips does something we disapprove of, a simple "no" does the trick.

The only exception to the "bad" word usage is for a certain dense bush in our yard that Chips likes to crawl into. He emerges a mess, covered with sticky leaves that take forever to pick out of his thick hair. But it isn't just the trouble of removing them or the aggravation of seeing him full of these dirty things that bothers us. The bush has many spiders, which sometimes bite him. Every time we see him headed there, one of us says "no," points to the bush and says "bad." He always complies with our wishes for the moment, but if we aren't there when he gets the idea, he conveniently forgets how forbidding that bush can be.

One night during Chips' first summer with us, Sam, while undressing, quickly pulls the belt from his chinos. Watching him, Chips drops his tail and runs away. Immediately, we understand that he's been hit or, at least threatened, with a belt. We both know that there's an especially bad place in hell for people who mistreat animals or children like that. Pity covers Sam's face.

"He's just a poor little guy," Sam tells me, now joining Chips' team permanently. I know that we both want to make up for whatever bad has happened to this dog, and give him a great time for the years he'll have with us.

"I don't want to think of my dog as a poor little guy, anymore. I want him to be strong, confident, carefree," I say. My mission – to make him a happy guy. I recall a documentary on TV about mothers and babies, demonstrating how babies thrived and gained confidence from their mothers' approval. They showed example after example of a mother smiling and paying attention to her baby. The child would react positively, laughing or smiling back. If the mother frowned or just didn't smile at the baby, his or her confidence faded until it became unhappy. If the mother continued her own dour expression, or turned her back on the baby and ignored him, the child always cried. Clearly, the sense of security and confidence, indeed the child's basic well being, depended on the mother's look of approval. Logically then, the same was true of dogs and their guardians. They watch us continuously. What they see in our faces instills confidence or insecurity.

Dogs seem to have an infinite capacity and incredible sensitivity to read human behavior and emotions. Obviously, Chips requires lots of approval to boost his shaky self image. And, approval, I promise myself, he would get. New resolutions are made. After the belt incident, we decide that Chips should receive all the reinforcement and kindness we could manage. I smile when looking at him and frequently tell him that he's "a good boy." No negatives are directed toward him unless his behavior endangers himself or someone else. We never leave or come home without saying something to him first. This idea was reinforced by Warren Eckstein. I remember one radio show when he talked about people who treated their dogs like pieces of furniture, walking by and ignoring them. That was not going to happen to our boy.

Sometimes, however, discipline cannot be avoided. A few months after adopting Chips we're riding in the car, with the window open so that he could enjoy the breeze. He sits on my lap in the front passenger seat. Sam, driving, stops at a red light. In an instant, Chips flies out the window in the middle of a street with traffic stopped. He has jumped to greet a passing Labrador. I can't believe that he survives that jump without injury. God was warning us. Sam's face darkens while pulling over. "You opened the window too much."

This situation certainly calls for a stern "no" from me. I get out of the car, administer the necessary harsh words in an appropriate tone and return with a suitably corrected Chips. After that, no more wide open car windows. But another problem soon surfaces – when a jogger or other person runs by us on our walks, Chips often leaps at the runner's leg. He doesn't do anything beyond the lunge, but Sam and I fear someone tripping or just getting angry about it. In litigious L.A., frivolous lawsuits constitute much of attorneys' time.

"You want mommy to get sued" I ask Chips. In addition to jumping on passing runners, he lurches after certain cars in the street, particularly pickup trucks. We again speculate about whether or not he'd been owned by a construction worker. Whatever his history, jumping on people's legs and pulling toward cars are dangerous habits that I know I have to immediately correct.

I call Michelle again to deal with the potential disaster and explain what happened. We would have to admit that we didn't take her advice on the separation anxiety. Would she resent it? I hope not.

"We don't want to take a chance on Chips getting even close to a moving car," I tell Michelle. Sam and I go with the trainer to a nearby, small park to teach Chips to come to us off leash in a public place. I have already accomplished that command in our backyard, but I soon learn that that's amateur stuff.

"When there are other distractions, like in a park" Michelle says, "commands are much harder for the dog to follow." We make some headway on "come" with a bunch of liver biscotti. Chips, however, turns his head toward any passing canine, male or female. Although he doesn't demonstrate the jumping or car lurches while Michelle is there, she suggests that when he does it to immediately take him by the chin, and say loudly into his face, "We don't do that." This scolding goes against my instincts, of course, but keeping Chips safe takes priority. I vow to do it next time he acts out. I don't have to wait too long.

The following month, I am walking on Lexington Avenue, in residential Beverly Hills, when Chips leaps on a runner's leg. The man turns around and scowls at me but doesn't break his stride. I administer the harsh words to Chips. After only a few instances of "we don't do that," he gets the message and the lurching pretty much stops. I think he's shocked by my tone and transformation into a disciplinarian. About once a year, for a few years, I have to remind him with the technique we learned that day.

There remains only one more circumstance in which Chips tries to lurch toward another individual. If he sees someone being injured or abused by someone else, he definitely wants to take on the abuser. I don't know exactly how he plans to do that because I never let him carry through on his efforts to go after anyone.

A few teenagers kidding around together walk in front of us one afternoon. When one boy playfully hits a girl over the head with a notebook, Chips tries to lunge after him. I think he would just have jumped. But, of course, I never let go of his leash to find out.

I remember only one time that I fear Chips might really act out aggressive feelings. After he becomes more protective of me, I am working with a volatile director on a script rewrite in my office. We argue all the time, as sometimes happens during rewrites.

"I think they should murder him!" The director becoming more unhinged than usual screams at me. Chips definitely does not like his tone. My protector looks the man directly in the eye and barks loudly at him. Getting red faced and louder the director ignores him,.

"They can't get rid of the body without being seen" I explain. But the director's face grows even redder, and his voice louder. Chips keeps barking until, frustrated that he's having no effect, walks slowly up to the man, now lighting a cigarette, and growls. Startled, the director stops yelling.

"I'm going out for a smoke" he says, backing away from my dog. Chips has really defused what was becoming an uncomfortable situation. I never cease to be amazed at how many ways Chips has become an asset. I sense, however, that he needs to do more. But what occupation can I provide? With unemployment figures rising for *our* species, what hope is there for my bored four legged charge?

Chapter 7

JOB HUNTING

If you pick up a starving dog and make him
prosperous, he will not bite you; that is the
principal difference between a man and a dog.

MARK TWAIN

Determined to transform Chips' sometimes depressed personality into a carefree spirit, I go out in the yard with him again and again, throw balls, sticks, squeaky toys. Then I usually retrieve them. I would make someone a wonderful pet. No doubt Chips possesses a more contemplative nature, operating on a higher plane than I do. After I demonstrate "fetch" over and over, he occasionally picks up a ball. However, bringing it back is not in his repertoire. After all, he doesn't see any humans chasing balls because he's never been to a baseball game. This is a deficit for which we're no doubt responsible. But my fantasies of backyard ballgames with him soon fade. A joyous canine bounding around the yard remains a remote vision.

The one exception to ball play happens when Sam and I play tennis. After our games, Chips' attention to balls definitely piques. We manage to find a court where we can take him with us. He stays quietly on the sidelines while we play, but when we finish he'll wiggle around and look at me as if to say – "My turn?" As usual, he wants to do what we're doing. When I see this expression, I throw the ball across the court; Chips turns into a speed demon, actually running after it, picking it up and bringing it back, at least somewhere in our vicinity. I throw and he chases again. Seeing him having normal dog fun, we begin throwing the ball each time we finish a game. These times are the only ones in which he'll condescend to chase a ball.

In time, Chips gains the audacity to sometimes walk outside my office door by himself, and briefly lie right there, in the sun, but only if I leave the door open. Once or twice he wanders into the backyard from there. Then Sam, who hates bugs indoors, and not knowing Chips has relocated outside and walked into the yard, invariably closes the door. The first time this happens we look around for Chips and realize that he's not in the house.

After a frantic search through every room and under and behind furniture,

I announce, "I think he's really gone." I just assume that if the door is closed, Sam must have brought our fur baby in. We walk to the door in question. Sure enough, there's Chips anxiously awaiting entry. He never barked to alert us. After this happens a few times, I decide that we need to teach him an effective way to communicate to us that he's locked out or get him his own set of keys. Having at one time been a teacher I thought to instruct by example. Chips watches as I go outside.

"Now close the door and walk away," I tell Sam. He does that. Then I get on all fours, (honestly) and "bark," at least what I construe as a bark. According to plan, Sam opens the door and pats my head. "You're a good girl." Chips watches all this rigmarole as we repeat it several times. Fortunately, none of our neighbors observe us. And we assume that Chips has learned the lesson.

"You got it," I ask him. But when, a day later, the wind closes the door, leaving Chips outside again, absolutely nothing has changed. "Why don't you bark?" I ask, almost expecting an answer, because I've noticed that his face is so expressive, he always looks on the verge of saying something. But he still never makes a sound when the door closes on him. He's picked up nada from our charade. We decide there and then that our little guy might not be Harvard material.

I still think Chips needs some kind of job. Though no backyard runner, he clearly wants exercise and loves to run, but apparently only when one of us is on the other end of the leash. He yearns to charge ahead on his walks. Both Sam and I try keeping up with him so he can run. But it's not possible for middle-agers to keep up with a ten or fourteen year old, which he is in dog years. When he spots a squirrel, his newly filled out, muscular, twenty-five pounds lunges full force after it. One day, Mr. C., as we sometimes call him, pulls so suddenly that I fall trying to keep up with him. As ungracefully as possible, I tumble, ripping my new jeans on the knee, but, hey, ripped jeans would be coming into style shortly. I'm just a trendsetter. When I recover, I vow to buy one of those long, extension leashes.

It isn't that correction or discipline hasn't occurred to us. It's just that it doesn't fit with our foremost mission –

making Chips happy. He wasn't a big dog whose strength would injure us. If we simply paid attention to what he was doing I knew I should be able to keep myself upright. At this point the initial training I do in the basics – "stay," "come," "sit," "down," and "give me five" is going well, so I see no point in denying Chips his natural pleasures. Ironically, whenever I say "give me five" he puts up his left paw to shake. Sam and I are both lefties; hence we take some pride in his natural adherence to the family trait.

Chips' main occupation consists of watching me all day long. Unlike some dogs I see, who play with their toys or run around the yard, he just lies in my office, looking bored, sighing and watching me write until I stop. His sometimes sad face melts my insides while I try to ignore it and work. I have a development deal with Nickelodeon, which has just opened a feature division. The script involves a story I'm passionate about concerning a man who taught high school for seventeen years, was a college graduate and became a multi-millionaire in the real estate business, all the while being totally illiterate. No one ever discovered his secret. My normal writing speed slows down, dissipated by Chips' needs. They must come first.

"Maybe he should have a job," I tell Sam. "You work, I work, but he has nothing to do."

"I could use some office help but I doubt if he knows my filing system. Why don't you train him to bring in the paper?" That sounded like a good idea. Then I wouldn't have to dash out in my bathrobe, hoping not to be seen by one of neighbors or, worse, a Tour of the Stars' Homes van.

I make a valiant attempt. "Chips, take this" I suggest, holding the newspaper out to him. Immediately he runs away from the extended paper, looking fearful, tucking his tail between his legs. Great. Someone obviously used a paper to whack him, probably during housebreaking. Chips doesn't mind the paper on a table, but has no use for rolled up ones. He wants nothing to do with our idea. "He'll have to find another job," I tell Sam.

One warm Sunday afternoon a couple of months after we adopt Chips, Sam's family comes by for a barbeque. We sit outside by the pool having drinks and hors d'ouvres. There's a piece of cheese under a cover on a small low table waiting to be consumed. My brother-in-law, Sammy, as distinguished from Sam, lifts the cover to take a piece, but Chips immediately begins barking at him. It's a display of confidence the likes of which our dog has never shown.

"It's not just for you," my brother-in-law says. Chips has now taken possession of our home, including the cheese. Every time Sammy goes for it, Chips barks right in front of him. After all, Chips had been introduced to cream cheese as his antibiotic delivery system. Now he must assume that all cheese belongs to his parents. But guarding the cheese is not a worthy profession, even for a dog. Fortunately, Sammy has a sense of humor and gets a kick out of the whole performance. I vow to keep Chips' obvious need for a real and worthy job in the back of my mind. If he doesn't find something useful to do, we might need that Prozac soon.

One afternoon Chips and I walk by the lovely, small park at Beverly Drive and Sunset where he likes to visit the koi pond. A commercial is being filmed there. Having once produced a low budget movie, I know how much every moment on the set costs, so I wait for them to finish a shot before walking by. The director thanks me. Then one of the crew begins talking to me about Chips and how photogenic he is. "I think he'd really do well in commercials."

"Yes, if he can be trained." The idea that Chips was photogenic had crossed my mind, of course, but he wasn't trained in many hand commands, which clearly dogs in TV, movies and commercials are.

"Here's the name of an agent for dogs," the young woman says, writing something on her card. "And here's the number of a trainer to call. I made the call to the trainer and explained who I was and where I'd gotten the number.

"It will take a few weeks. He can either stay with us or you can bring him every day." Staying with them was, naturally, out of the question. We didn't even like leaving Chips with his Aunt Berta when we <u>had</u> to go out of town.

Taking him every day was a big time commitment, but she said it was no more than an hour. "The dogs can only absorb so much at once."

"Oh, I'll bring him every day." My little pumpkin, a movie star! Chips might finally feel the satisfaction of having a job, something more interesting than just lying in my office. This time it would actually be a job with pay. He could finally begin to cover his bills. Fantasies of filet mignon on the set, custom made raincoats and private planes to take him to locations danced in my head.

The following week Chips and I drive to Culver City to meet the trainer. "Hi Chips" the woman trainer chirps after being introduced. "Now, you sit over there mom," she says, pointing me to a chair. "And I'll show you the kind of training we do." She takes Chips' leash and tried to lead him away. He immediately digs in his feet and looks at me.

"It's o.k." I tell him. By now the woman is dragging him by his leash across the floor. When she stops, he tries to pull back to me. I pop up and go to Chips. "Why don't you just tell me what to do and I'll train him?"

"That's impossible. He has to respond to a trainer on the set and hand commands from that person. Actually, it would be better if you'd wait outside. Then he won't be distracted." I hesitate.

"You don't use punishment, do you?"

"No, only rewards."

"O.K. You're gonna like this Chips" I tell him with a pat on the head. "It involves treats. Mommy come back soon," and I walk through the door. Within no more than two minutes, I hear whining. Steeling myself not to rush in, I sit there waiting for the whining to disappear. A moment later the whining can no longer be heard. Good, he's settled down, I think. Two minutes later I hear barking. It doesn't stop. The door opens.

"I'm afraid he's too attached to you. He won't give me his attention but keeps looking at the door. If you want, I can take him to our facility for two weeks and see if he can be trained there."

"I don't think he'd like that."

She paused. "To be honest, I don't either."

"Thanks anyway." Chips would never know the pleasures of stardom and I'd never have the delight of handling his trust fund. Oh, well. Back to job hunting.

Chapter 8

NO SEX IN THE CITY

---

*A dog has lots of friends because he
wags his tail and not his tongue.*

UNKNOWN

Six months pass. Nickelodeon has closed its feature division and my development deal along with it. I now have another development deal at A&E on the teacher story. Naturally, they want a rewrite. I'm busy with that while Sam begins winding down his business in Palo Alto. At the same time we speculate on Chips' sex life. Is he a virgin? As he isn't neutered, he may have known the pleasures of the flesh. My first visit to the dog park with him confirms his interest. Chips goes right up to the largest, most ferocious looking male Rottweiler there and climbs his rump to hump him. O.K. He's probably gay. That's fine with us, but I'm not sure the other dog feels the same way. I dash after Chips, fearing for his life.

Fortunately, the recipient of my dog's attentions appears quite mellow, barely acknowledging his fruitless efforts. Other than this one foray, Chips doesn't partake in normal dog park activities. It soon becomes apparent, however, that he's interested in humping either sex. Bisexual for sure. When not initiating a liaison, he explores the periphery of the park to pee where others have before. The romping and playing I expect never happens.

Chips' humping extends to almost every dog, regardless of sex, who visits us. His sexual instincts remain intact despite the fact that he has something called cryptorchidism, where one or both testicles are undescended. In his case it's one. In fact, the condition, I learn, produces more testosterone than normal, so excessive humping comes with the territory.

We know that responsible pet guardians neuter their dogs while they're young, but we decided to wait until Chips' health and proper weight were restored to normal. Sam in the meantime has begun to wonder what it would be like to have Chips' puppy.

"Are you kidding? Remember how many organizations we support which are trying to find homes for all the unwanted dogs and cats around?" Sending checks, neutering our own and adopting other animals are all most of us can do to help.

"You're right." But our little guy is over two years old, an adolescent, and hasn't yet been fixed. His favorite pastime seems to be licking his penis and single testicle. "You're talking about removing one of the only two toys he plays with," Sam argues. Saying that Sam now takes a personal interest in Chips understates the case. Nonetheless, I know it's important to neuter the dog, having urged many others to do the same.

One day a visiting friend asks us, "How would you feel knowing Chips would be sexually frustrated for the rest of his life? After all you aren't providing any liaisons, are you?" That does it. We know the necessity of committing to the nasty deed shouldn't be put off another moment.

"What about a vasectomy? Could they do it and remove one testicle, the one that was undescended, and leave the other for him to lick" Sam asks.

"Maybe, or we could ask about Neuticals?" I'd read about these imitation testicles that can be inserted into the sack after removing the testicles. Unbelievable but true. Sam reluctantly goes with me to the vet to discuss, just discuss, these options. Never mind that the adoption fee we paid included the surgery. We want to make sure that our boy has the best surgeon for this procedure. Through references, we have located a highly regarded surgeon and tell him, "We prefer a vasectomy." He refuses to do that, insisting that castration is the way to go.

"It will calm him down, prevent prostate cancer and incontinency later on." The extra testosterone in dogs with undescended testicles apparently makes them more prone to prostate cancer than normal.

"What about Neuticals" I ask the doctor.

"What is that?" He has never used nor heard of such a thing. While I explain, the expression on his face indicates that he finds this idea not only unthinkable but ludicrous. Very reluctantly, we agree to go along with his recommendation. Sam still views the prospect of Chips' surgery with even more distaste than I. But no doubt it's the right thing to do.

Nervously, we deliver Chips for the morning procedure. The doctor comes out a few minutes after taking Chips in to tell us that one of his teeth is rotted. "As long as he's unconscious, the tooth should really be removed. Why don't you come see it."

We go in the operating room where Chips, already out cold, is lying on what looks like a rack. We examine the tooth, agree to the removal, then turn to the technician who has electric clippers in hand. "Please be careful clipping him," I say. The technician doesn't say, "sure" or "don't worry" or anything, which should have been a warning.

When we take Chips home later that day, the surgery looks o.k., but he begins to lick his penis, which sheath has been shaved, despite the fact that the surgery was not anywhere near it. We're appalled. Chips begins crying after a few hours. We manage to hide a pain pill in his food. He falls asleep after taking it, but soon wakes up, continues the licking and crying. By the next day, his organ is getting swollen. On further examination we see that the flesh there has been slightly nicked. We are furious, especially as there was no necessity for shaving the hair in that specific area. We call the doctor. Sam goes to pick up an antibiotic for what looks like an infection.

After another day, the antibiotics aren't working and Chips, still miserable, cries intermittently. The penis grows redder and more swollen. We worry and get even angrier that our dog has been subjected to this needless suffering. Sam, heading for a business meeting in the same direction as the vet, first stops with me and Chips to see him. He walks into the vet's office and asks for the doctor to come out to the car to examine Chips.

"The doctor is preparing for surgery and can't see him now" the receptionist tells him.

Always soft spoken and polite to a fault, Sam, anything but a confrontational type, has turned into Chips' protector as surely as I have. "Let me assure you that I'm not leaving this waiting room until the doctor sees what's happened to our dog," he says. Making this fuss in the waiting room does nothing to enhance business. Sam knows this. In another moment, the doctor comes outside to the car and examines our boy. He agrees that the infection doesn't look good, then gives us a new antibiotic and a plastic Victorian collar for Chips to wear so that he won't lick the area.

We hate putting this big, hard plastic thing on Chips' head as much as he hates wearing it. With the sharp edged collar sticking out, he bangs into walls and furniture, has difficulty drinking water and sleeping. It looks like a vaudeville act, but I am not amused.

"Why can't they make these things more comfortable?" I ask, covering the edge of the collar with surgical tape to blunt the sharpness a little. I'm surprised that no one has invented an improvement on this contraption. During the day, when Chips stays with me, I leave the collar off because I can easily monitor his attempts to lick. But at night, the poor thing must sleep with his head inside of the plastic cone. He looks like an unhappy circus performer.

In a few days, the new antibiotic works, the collar gets put away and Chips recovers. But watching him suffer has almost done us in. For the first time in my life, I write a scathing letter. In it, I tell the vet how we feel about the unnecessary shaving. I also point out that no matter how great a surgeon he is, he's really "only as good as his worst technician," the proverbial chain being only as strong as its weakest link.. That technician caused enough of a problem so that the doctor's excellent work was obscured in the whole trying experience.

Much to my surprise, the surgeon writes back to say that we are absolutely right, and that the tech no longer works there. From then on, he explains, they are hiring "only licensed veterinary technicians." I am shocked that such an upscale veterinary practice has anything but. If these veterinarians do that, pity the poor animals at the less demanding facilities. The doctor also includes a check for the extra visit to change Chips' antibiotic. I appreciate his honesty, but none of it changes the misery that Chips has endured, which matters most to us.

After all the healing, our dog looks surprised and disappointed a few times when he goes to lick the former pleasure center. But within a short time, he adjusts. However, someone else doesn't. A few months after the surgery, I come home to find Sam on the floor examining Chips, who has assumed his frequent on-his-back, let-it-all-hang-out position.

"Darling, look what's happened. He's got nothing left!" Sam informs me of what I've already noticed – Chips' smallish penis had shrunk to half its original size.

"He's not bothered by it." But I can see that Sam definitely is. Chips' sexual instincts are still intact as he always humps my leg when certain people come to visit. I know all the experts say this habit's not sexual but a desire for domination. All the same, to those watching it still looks sexual.

Speaking of sex, B.C. – Before Chips, I fantasized our own post dog love life being no problem. I figured that we'd just put the dog in the backyard while romance was in the air. There he'd romp and play innocently while we had private time inside. But who knew we'd get Mr. Insecurity, who doesn't like going anywhere we aren't...ever. So, unless we want lots of crying and all the French doors' glass scratched, we have to leave Chips in the house. To close the bedroom door is to make love to a chorus of whimpers and door scratches. Our only remaining option: let him watch. That's right – as in a front row seat.

Unlike many dogs we've heard about, Chips does not try to get on the bed or interfere. Some dogs actually try to get between the partners. Chips, with better judgement, just watches. We try to forget about him. Sam is better at this than I. He assures me I'll get used to it, but I don't have that confidence. One day, after we have him a month, I come up with a scheme for a lovely, intimate afternoon.

"We'll put Chips in the kitchen, leave through the back room, go into the garage, open the garage door as we do when we drive out, close the garage, walk quietly through the side gate and sneak back in through my open office door. All the noises will imply that we're leaving." Then, I figured, we'd take off our shoes, tiptoe back through the entry and silently creep up the stairs to our bedroom. There, we'd try to keep our activities as quiet as possible. This was worse than living with your parents.

We go through this entire scenario, come in the side door, take off our shoes and begin up the stairs, which did not creek. Just as we got to the second step, Chips begins his baleful wailing and howling in the kitchen. Either he smells us, hears us or has that incredible canine intuition. But up we went anyway, intent on our plan. We can't stand the dog's frustration. We laugh at what we've done. It is the last time our guy is closed out of anything.

When Chips first joined the family we designated our bed as a private domain. At the beginning of our relationship with him, it was never a problem. Someone had obviously trained him to stay off the bed. In the morning he'd merely puts his paws up on my side and looks to see if we were sleeping. Sweetly, he didn't wake us, never barked or jumped up to get us going.

"This is great" I tell Sam. "We maintain some privacy and won't encourage him to change. But we have no real privacy anyway, so we begin to urge him to join us on the bed while we read, watch television or sleep. Chips, however, remains very reluctant to come up, probably assuming punishment will follow. With time and repeated coaxing, however, he ultimately comes up, always staying near the foot of the bed. He seemed to want to be able to take off at a moment's notice. In no time at all we undo all of his early training.

We want to do nothing to discourage Chips' growing assertiveness, so out of character for the skinny, retiring canine we adopted. Naturally, it's very easy for a guardian to stop or insist on any behavior with harsh words and actions, pushing around an impotent creature, whose total life is in his/her control. But we're not trying for a little robot to perform all sorts of meaningless actions for the satisfaction of the master's ego. Fortunately, Sam and I are of one mind on this –- our purpose on earth, at this time and place, is to make one dog happy. Newer challenges, however, in unchartered territory were ahead.

Chapter 9

THE GROOMING WARS

---

*Anybody who doesn't know what soap
tastes like never washed a dog.*

FRANKLIN P. JONES

Tibetan Terriers are high maintenance. Although they have hair instead of fur, and shed only a few puffs once a year, their thick, sometimes wavy double coat gets easily matted, needs daily brushing, and grows fast. Add the dog's intermittent chewing on himself to that formula and you have a scraggly mess in no time. A couple of months after his hair grows in, Chips definitely needs a haircut. We want to take care of his grooming ourselves, and prefer a shorter puppy cut that requires less maintenance. Neither of us cares for fancy "foo-foo cuts," as Sam dubs them, which some "owners" like. The bathing we could manage, but using scissors on Chips' face or clippers on his nails becomes risky on a wriggly, energetic pooch sporting black nails. Where the quick of the nail ends is difficult to determine. We consider a groomer, then obtain a recommendation.

The first time at the groomer, Sam and I go together. Whenever Sam senses possible danger to Chips, he's right there, being as protective as possible. We notice that this emporium and all similar grooming places have small cages they put the dogs in while they await their baths, and when they're already groomed. That wasn't for our little boy. A cage to him meant the shelter. I call to find out when Chips could be taken right away so that he needn't be confined. We would, of course, wait for him.

"Be here at 7.30," I'm told. No problem. I've always kept my mornings free for writing. The A&E script is not quite finished, but for Chips my schedule would naturally be revised. We arrive at the grooming place where I start to explain how sensitive and nervous our dog can be. But before three words are out, Chips gets a cookie shoved in his mouth and is whisked away. Thirty-five dollars later, a magnificent, handsome, clean, angelic looking creature returns to us. Immediately, I purchase a roll of film.

Luckily I record his idyllic look for posterity because the following day, Chips, on a bold ten minute foray into our backyard alone, comes in looking like a raccoon, with damp black earth stuck all over his previously immaculate white mouth. My thrill over his pristine cleanliness is gone in one short garden dig, probably in search if the rawhide he'd buried. No amount of washing with water and soap gets all the dirt off. The white mustache now stays a definite gray.

We bathe Chips ourselves in between grooming visits. Although no lover of water, our boy seems less reluctant to be bathed by us than the groomer. But he lets me know that the worst thing is having his ears and face wet. He squirms around madly on the towels trying to get those things dry right away. I learn quickly to use the dryer on those parts first, to calm him down some. Sitting still to be dried requires incredible patience on his part and determination on mine. When he's seventy-five percent done, I open the door to the bathroom where I've locked him in, and he races around like a madman, actually playing with whatever toy he stumbles upon first. This, in fact, is the only time that he ever, ever plays with toys. I'm not sure if he's trying to finish the drying au naturalle or he's just exuberant being let out of the small drying space.

Having learned that we almost never scold, and that our efforts always try to improve his situation, Chips trusts us more and more as time goes by. The dropping of his head when approached greatly diminishes. A confidence we are determined to instill in him begins to show.

After a half dozen visits to that first groomer, I notice Chips is ever more unwilling to go there. Also, we don't like the idea of people handling him out of our sight; we can't see the back area where the dogs are actually groomed. After one particular visit, Chips and I are out front, heading for my car, when one of the groomers comes out for a smoke. Chips, who by now has definitely become more secure, begins barking aggressively at this unfriendly looking woman. I decide that not knowing exactly what is behind his obvious dislike of her, it might be a good idea to switch groomers. That turns out to be a fortunate idea – my brother-in-law's dog was later greatly harmed by this place when some groomer got and left soap in his eye, which nearly blinded him.

The same day that Chips lets me know that the groomer is on his s___ list, I spot what looks like a beautiful blond Tibetan Terrier walking with a pleasant looking man a few blocks from our house. We stop to meet them and ask where she's groomed.

"I'll take your number and have my wife call you. She's in charge of grooming." One could naturally expect a Beverly Hills resident to be reluctant to give his phone number to a stranger. As promised, we get a call and are told that their Tibetan Terrier was groomed in one of those special trucks that comes to your house. These services are practically de rigeur for our neighborhood anyway. The next time Chips needs grooming, we will call the recommended woman.

In about a month, Chips turns into a mess again. The new mobile groomer pulls into our driveway with her big white van. "Can I be inside the truck while you groom him?"

"It's too small," she tells me, "and the dogs are better behaved if the owner isn't there." This mantra we would hear over and over from vets, groomers, technicians, and anyone else from whom Chips felt he must protect himself.

I reluctantly carry him into the truck, instruct the woman to "please cut out the mats in the hair. Don't try untangling them," which would obviously hurt while they were being pulled. It's incredible to me that anyone would try to do it the painful way, but they do. An hour later, Chips is returned, again looking fantastic. No harm seems to have been done to him, and his black and white plume, always my best gauge of whatever was going on with him, once again wags.

We make a big fuss over Chips, and offer him treats so that he likes the "afterglow" of the experience, if not the process itself. But as time goes by his anxiety about grooming worsens. Every time the truck shows up, he starts whining and shaking. Whenever we are out and about town together he barks ferociously at any grooming truck with the elevated, uniquely shaped top. Even a solid white non-grooming van or truck earns his wrath. We loathe putting him in the van even more than he hates going, but we simply cannot manage the entire grooming procedure ourselves. The groomer never seems to harm him, and I keep my ears open for any crying or barking that might occur. It never does. Also, I peek through the window now and then to make sure that Chips gets the treatment he obviously deserves.

"He's fine as soon as you leave," the groomer assures me. About a year later, this nice groomer breaks her arm and turns her business over to employees. We do not trust the others as we trusted her. We must find another good groomer.

Karen, highly recommended by my dog loving hairdresser, has a grooming place in Venice, by the beach. It's about a forty minute drive there, but for Chips we obviously dismiss the extra time involved. He needs his easily matted hair cut. We get to the shop as Karen finishes another dog. "You can help me wash him if you like" she tells me. I like her already.

"Sure." I'll see exactly how she handles Chips. First she introduces herself to Chips, which I love, instead of just grabbing him, as many would. In an elevated, large sink we begin bathing him together while Sam watches. Karen's placed a rubber restraining loop around Chips neck so we can take off his collar. After a moment of our four hands shampooing him, he's covered with suds. Karen gets a phone call. "I'll just see who it is and be right back."

"No problem." As she turns to go, Chips suddenly jumps out of the sink and is hanging by his neck in the stretched out loop! A nanosecond goes by while I grasp the situation, then grab a dog rump, getting him back into the sink. I didn't breathe for a moment while realizing that my dog almost hung himself right in front of me. Sam, witnessing this whole thing, can't believe what's happened.

"How did he get away from you!?"

"He just jumped a few inches beyond me." I think he's all right." Sam could see that the dog hadn't turned blue. Under all that hair of course we wouldn't know if he did.

Karen comes back, gets the scoop on what she's missed and helps me finish. "I've just lost my lease. That call was my landlord." Oh, no. I really like this groomer. "But don't worry. I'm getting a truck and can come to your place. I'll call when I'm set up."

"Fine." She then trims Chips' hair into a puppy cut and gets the hair out of his eyes. With our dog's new haircut, bouncy walk and unusually expressive face and eyes, we are constantly, and I mean constantly, stopped by people wanting to know "what kind of dog is that?" Or they say, "it's a person's face," assuming this was the highest compliment you could pay a dog. When asked about his breed, I'm reluctant to tell them because I'd be encouraging a lot of folks to go to Tibetan Terrier breeders. I am a true believer in the saying of one Los Angeles rescue group – "Don't breed or buy, while animals in shelters die." Sam now believes that too, so we usually just say "he's a terrier mix, from the pound." If they say that their own dogs are adopted from the pound or a rescue group, then we naturally tell them the truth.

After Karen gets her truck, not some slick, new, grooming van you'd expect in these parts, but a ramshackle, old, patched together job, it comes clunking into our driveway so that she can again groom Chips. We like her even more as time passes because of her gentle handling of our boy and letting me into the truck with her and her always present rescue dogs. These change, depending on whether she finds homes for them or keeps them herself. Chips' dislike of grooming does not dissipate despite Karen's careful, affectionate handling. He heads for the "hole" anytime she pulls up, but at least I know he's being treated the right way.

During the days following hurricane Katrina, Karen wants to go down South to help groom the dogs rescued in the floods. She needs money for a plane ticket to get there. We could imagine the anxiety and worry of people forced to abandon their pets in order to be rescued themselves. We and another of Karen's customers were able to buy the ticket so that she could help out there for one long weekend. When Karen returned, she gave us an album of photos of the dogs she had groomed.

Thank God Chips never needs any other groomer. In between haircuts we bathe him ourselves, either in the shower or in the bathtub. Each has its advantages and deficits. When Chips sees his shampoo and conditioner come out, he immediately hides under a bench upstairs. After prying him out, I carry or push him into the bathroom, in an effort to preserve what's left of my back.

Even for two people, this dog bathing remains a messy, exhausting job involving soap and water, always shaken off Chips onto us, anti-itch conditioners that have to set while he tries to jump out of the tub, at least six towels, dryers, brushes and a lot of energy. I collapse on the bed afterward to admire my hard won results. Chips looks incredibly handsome while I've now been transformed into one of those island reality show survivors where there's been no human grooming of any real sort for a month. At least I've got my priorities straight.

Chapter 10

COYOTE BLUES

If you pick up a starving dog and make him prosperous, he will not bite you; that is the principal difference between a man and a dog.

MARK TWAIN

Actually, sleeping in the Hills of Beverly can be an eerie and less than glamorous affair. On a few nights, especially in summer, when the hills are parched by lack of rain, the coyotes come down lower than normal and can be heard devouring the stray cats and small dogs who may have walked out for a pee through their doggy doors. There's this horrible screaming for a few seconds followed by silence. We know that at times the coyotes travel in pairs or trios so that they can even take on larger dogs. One man we heard about in another neighborhood was actually walking his dog on a leash when a coyote ran by and grabbed the leash right out of his hand.

Sam's brother's Bichon Frisee was attacked by one of these animals in her own backyard at night. The poor dog had gone out for a pee, gotten mauled and dragged herself back through her doggy door with her throat ripped open. She made it through emergency surgery the next morning, but had been subjected to a terrible trauma. The police told my brother-in-law that coyotes can jump twelve feet high from a standing position, so having a fence on one's property is not a deterrent. They suggest getting pepper spray or carrying a golf club while going out with the dog at night. Of course we immediately get both. But knowing how handy we aren't, the likelihood is that we will douse ourselves or Chips by misusing the pepper spray. The golf club, more low tech, appears something we can both likely handle.

At night, we begin taking Chips out together, and rarely in the hills. If we do, one of us carries a baseball bat or golf club. One hot night, as we start down the street, there's a particularly large coyote walking toward us from the corner. Sam's ahead of me with the club. Chips, who always wants to greet other dogs, nonetheless must sense that this is not the right opportunity for socializing. He and I stand still; then I begin backing up, my gaze never leaving the coyote. Sam brandishes the club around while backing up toward our house himself. I yell, "Don't come one step closer!" with all the bravado I can muster. Somehow all of this nonsense works. The coyote stands right where he is, probably more amused than scared by this odd threesome.

Despite the coyotes' gruesome killings, their obvious hunger makes me feel sorry for them. With no one to feed them, they simply have to rely on small animals for their sustenance. Chips, however, now twenty-six pounds, would not be one of them if I could help it. After that night with the coyote on our block, we never let Chips into the backyard alone in the dark. Even if it's raining, during which a great deal of coaxing is needed to get him out the door, his last pee is always accompanied or watched from the doorway by one of us, where we can run out if an attacker appears.

As time goes by, Chips grows more stubborn about going into the rain. Even if I force him out, he'll often sit against the door getting drenched instead of doing what he's there for. It's pathetic. And though I always dry him when he comes in, he still refuses to budge. I know what that means – a middle of the night wake up for me, when even the best bladder no longer can wait. I soon catch on to the fact that if I show Chips the towel first, he will deign to run out and take care of business, secure that he'll be dried off immediately.

Most often, if we walk him after dark, it's on the commercial part of Rodeo Drive, with street and store lights. We have to drive the car down to town, but it pays – Chips feels right at home as he prances by the long, lit up windows of the most fashionable stores. Yes, he actually prances like he's in some show ring. What more quintessential arena was there for a Beverly Hills dog to walk?

Nightly, Chips now comes on the bed and visits us, enjoying the moments of full attention to him, without the distraction of our daytime obligations. If I pick up a book or newspaper to read, he moves closer, places his paws over the reading material, and looks right into my eyes. There's no resisting this. "O.K., so I'll read in ten or fifteen years." He cocks his head to one side as if trying to understand my words. No doubt about it – he wants to comprehend, interact, have more intimacy, but doesn't know exactly how. Neither do I.

Looking into Chips' eyes, there's no denying his intense desire to understand and communicate. His silence and obvious interest give him some of the same qualities as a psychoanalyst. Listening with absolute attention is something people pay psychotherapists and psychiatrists a lot of money to do. The dogs don't comment on what we say, but the listening and interest alone have their obvious high value.

Sometimes the solitude of a dog, his inability to speak to those he's closest to, boils over into a kind of frustrated cry or mew. At night on our bed, Chips, for instance, picks up his foot and reaches it out, then down, touching my hand. I am, like every one of my species, helpless to bridge this gap, erase his isolation except by trying to fulfill his needs and desires. I respond with a few words of encouragement, a head scratch, and a hug. He answers with a look of adoration that no one deserves.

All day, our dog, like others of his kind, waits patiently while I write and do all the tasks humans spend their time on, and which dogs, doubtless, don't understand. But it's for the reward of affection and attention that they all yearn. If I'm distracted and fail to give Chips this kind of regard at night, he leaves the bed, clearly hurt, and literally turns his back to us from his own bed. To him, attention clearly equals love or at least respect, which he needs, which all dogs need. Hell, it's what we all need. If there was ever any doubt about this, I only had to look or smile at my boy to get his tail immediately swishing.

I agree with what J.R. Ackerley writes in MY DOG TULIP, (New York: Poseidon, 1987) "What strained and anxious lives dogs must lead, so emotionally involved in the world of men, whose affection they strive endlessly to secure, whose authority they are expectedly unquestioningly to obey, and who's mind they can never do more than imperfectly reach and comprehend."

Despite Chips' nightly visits to our bed, when we turn out the lights, he jumps off and returns to his own pillow bed, in the corner where the chair used to be. That's been moved to make room for Chips' bed with a view of his parents. I guess he leaves because he's had enough of us. But Sam misses a dog sleeping with him at night, in a kind of warm family setup, the way he used to have with Daisy. Nonetheless, we can't seem to convince our pooch that we're worth sleeping with.

One day we buy Chips a big donut bed with soft sides, which he immediately climbs in and takes possession of. When it first arrives by UPS, we see it's not the color that we ordered, which blends with the color of our bedroom. Nonetheless, we put it down and decide to mail it back for an exchange the next day. But after one night, when we fold the bed into its box, our former orphan climbs on top and won't get off. "You're not taking my new bed away" he's clearly telling us. Color coordination doesn't interest him. What the heck? So the color's wrong. We aren't going to remove, even for a few days, what Chips has already made his. Reopening the box, we put the bed back in its rightful place. Chips steps into it, as he does every night from then on. In time Sam and I begin to feel rejected – "We're the only two people in America who <u>want</u> a dog to sleep with them and can't get him to," I say. But the object is to make Chips happy, right? If he's chosen his donut bed over us, so be it.

"You notice how he always likes to go under things," Sam observes one day. The bench, the desk. He probably would crawl under our bed if it was high enough. I bet he'd love a roof for his bed."

"Probably." I know that den animals like that sort of thing. Although my husband's a licensed mechanical engineer, he's decidedly unhandy.

"I'm better at the theoretical," he explains. So he asks the handyman we use if he could build something simple to go over Chips' bed. With holed clapboard and thin piping the handyman puts together a top, three sides and supports. He paints it the color of the bedroom, lines it with some paper to cover the rough sides, and, voila'! Chips has a four poster over his donut. If he liked the bed before, he's now mad for it.

Chips still deigns to hop up on our bed with us before lights out. And since we encourage it, we could no longer be annoyed if he wants to come up when the romantic mood strikes. But sex with a dog on the bed is too much even for dog lovers like us. We start telling him, "go back to sleep," when we want him to leave the premises. Given his sensitivity, Chips gets the message right away, and takes off. But, uncannily, as the years pass, he senses when we're thinking of such things. Maybe it's the music we sometimes put on. As soon as he hears Frank Sinatra, Chips positions himself right there on the bed, staring at us, as if to say, "I want to be part of this too, guys."

Usually, a few hugs followed by, "Go back to sleep" does the trick. "Is our sex life really worth offending him" I ask Sam one night. He does a double take, not sure if I'm kidding.

Rainy days give me the biggest headache. Chips refuses to go to the bathroom and get wet no matter how many times I try to let him out. After a whole day of pulling the same stunt he has to be uncomfortable. I decide to drive him down to town. It's nighttime, winter. Back and forth we trudge in the parking garage behind Little Santa Monica Boulevard as it pours and thunders outside. Chips has obviously decided that it's too wet out to pee. Can't say I don't sympathize. I remember an overnight tent trip from summer camp involving an outhouse in the middle of a rainy night. Not fun. And that had an indoor toilet!

In my rain gear, I've carried him to the car, driven down to town and tried to walk him outside. He will have none of it, digging in his feet, then sitting. So I've walked the few steps down to the garage behind the stores because I'm panicking; he hasn't gone since morning. Desperate times, desperate measures and all that. "You go pee pee right now" I order as authoritatively as I know how. He looks at me as if to ask, "Where's the toilet?!"

Not a pristine structure, the garage is rather a concrete floored affair, opened at both ends, where water drips in. "Right now," I tell him, figuring one pee here will not do much to change the nature of the place. If the meter maids or guys checking on cars see us they may alert the police, but even in Beverly Hills the cops have better things to do with their time than ticket a dog guardian whose dog is "soiling" the garage. Dutifully, the little guy keeps his nose to the ground, sniffing, sniffing as conscientiously as he can, but finds no suitable place. I trek from one end to the other, imagining that if this doesn't work, Chips' bladder might burst, necessitating an emergency clinic visit. That will amount to a fortune in bills, and possibly end by plastering my picture in the "Beverly Hills Courier" for being an abusive pet parent who never takes out her dog "to do his business."

After fifteen minutes, I decide enough is enough. "I'm not going" his body language tells me, but out I pull him in his harness, down Rodeo Drive, past all the famous designer stores. At least he's sporting one of his two raincoats, and I stick my umbrella out to cover him. My getting wet clearly remains irrelevant at this point. But as soon as we're close to a store, he ducks into the drier entry way, looking at me as if I'm Cruella Deville to subject him to these conditions. Never mind that I'm soaking wet by now. "You have to at least go pee pee," I insist, leading him over to a tree several yards away. Finally, at the second tree he lifts his leg one long time. After that and a dash by him into Prada's large protected entryway, I know that any additional efforts on his part are out of the question.

I drive home regretting that my outing to buy dog rain boots that afternoon failed. "He's so sweet" muttered the salesgirl who'd helped me place medium-sized booties on his four hairy paws. "With these on it won't be hard to clean him up when he comes in all wet."

"And this is no water loving Retriever" I tell her. Thinking how much nicer it'll be for Chips not to muddy up his paws in the rain, I'm ready to make the purchase when he simply raises one paw at a time and shakes off each carefully placed booty. They don't come in precise sizes so the fit's rather poor. So much for dry feet. I know that dogs like to touch the ground with their paws anyway because the scent glands reside there. They can leave their mark just by pawing the ground – men don't have it that easy.

Finally at home, I peel off Chips' soaking raincoat, which he can't get rid of fast enough. He gives a good shake to make sure that I'm as wet as possible before rubbing his head on the carpet, trying to dry his ears in our little back room. "Yes, I'll be right with you" I tell him, taking off my own coat and shoes. I grab the small dryer kept there for just such moments, sit next to the hairy mess and begin drying. First the ears – what he most hates wet – then the head and face, before working my way down to his soaking legs and paws.

Chips turns his head this way and that, relishing every bit of the warm air as I run my hands under and around his thick coat, lifting and rubbing it to dry faster. I know that sometime during the night, preferably when I'm deep asleep and having some immensely fascinating dream, I'll hear him walking around, hoping to rouse me to take him down because the time has come – rain or no rain, when he can't wait another moment. And sure enough, at 2:20 A.M., even Chips cannot hold things any longer.

I hurry down the stairs after him to turn off the alarm and let him into the yard. It's still pouring. When he sees the rain, he hesitates just a second before plunging into the downfall to do what should have taken place hours ago. I know that if I have a towel waiting in my hands he'll be grateful and I will save my rug in the den from muddy paw prints. When he's finished he runs back to me.

I wrap him in the towel I've found while he's out, pick the soggy package up and dry him in the back room for the third time today. I'm exhausted but amazed that I don't resent it. That's saying a lot for someone who hates to be awakened. I guess it's the tail wagging back and forth and his doggy smile while I dry him that must make it all worthwhile. But as the moments pass, I start to nod off. He paws me awake. I turn off the dryer and together we climb the stairs to our respective beds. My husband's sleep remains undisturbed.

Chapter 11

THE WELL TRAINED GUARDIAN

Properly trained, a Man can be Dog's best friend.

COREY FORD

Everyone knows that when you get a dog, some kind of training is in order. And in no time flat, Chips has the both of us whipped into perfect shape. Apparently, you can teach a middle aged "owner" new tricks. When we first adopted him, Chips didn't come near us while we were eating. "This is great. Don't feed him from the table," I told Sam. But my husband fixed that situation in short order.

"How many pleasures does he really have?" Seeing Chips sniffing the air at the first food aroma, Sam began giving him little bits of whatever we were eating, assuming it isn't tamales, curried chicken or the like. And nothing with sauce or strong seasoning of course. In the blink of an eye, Chips had Sam performing on command. Now, when the meal begins, he stations himself right next to Sam's chair, sitting and turning his adorable face up, waiting to catch Sam's eye. Much of the time, Chips just watches the floor, perhaps expecting someone to throw food on it. Did he live with a baby in his previous life? Did they just throw his food on the floor? This looking down for food is a habit he never outgrows.

If Sam doesn't succumb in the first few minutes, Chips begins pawing him. Then, either Sam relents or says to me "What do I do?" or "Have you got something for him?" I assure him that Chips has just completed a generous meal, always consisting of some cooked meat or chicken, usually a vegetable and always some kibble. But the man can't stand the dog's pleading ways.

"I'm not getting into this. You created the problem." If Sam can't or doesn't think he should feed Chips what he's eating, he reluctantly gets up and gives him some treat, which does nothing to discourage the dog's determination. If Chips comes around to my chair, I simply say "mommy hungry too," and give him the same pathetic look he gives me. The absence of forthcoming food helps him soon grasp the meaning of that phrase, though I admit to weakening myself at times. If I'm eating something sure to make him sick I say, "No good for doggies." The idea of just saying the word "no" to him never crosses either of our minds. After all, we were in the confidence building business.

As Sam grows less resistant, Chips, a quick study, grows bolder. But unlike other dogs we know, he never takes food that isn't given to him, unless it falls on the floor. And though easy for him to do, he never grabs a sandwich off the table when no one is looking, as our friend's dog does. Instead, Chips possesses a delicacy and refinement beyond the norm for his species. Sam has the identical sensibility and, much like Chips, prefers things in small pieces. Give Sam a sandwich and he'll cut it into four sections; even corn on the cob is knifed off into kernels and put on the plate.

Give Chips a large cookie and he'll place it down and look at you, hoping you have the good sense to pick it up and break it into pieces. If not, he'll eventually struggle to do it himself. If he can't break the treat, he won't eat it until some human is bright enough to figure out what must be done. No rough and ready, gobble-anything-down pooch he. "How did you make it on the streets for even one day?" I ask him.

As the years of meals go by, Chips decides that if Sam has the gall to ignore him or actually say, "not for doggies," he just removes Sam's napkin from his lap and runs around with it, or begins chewing it right there. It's not done in a mean or aggressive way, but with a sense of play. It always makes us laugh. And, yes, I am sure that dogs have a sense of humor. You can even see in some of their interaction that they tease each other and their humans, hiding things from them, running off with toys and other objects. If Chips wants some interaction while we sit and eat, he just goes back and forth under our knees, rubbing himself as he goes.

As to manners, Chips' politeness extends to wiping off his mouth after eating. Immediately following a meal, he drinks water. His mustache, beard and sometimes his ear tips get wet. In time I notice that he proceeds at these junctures to the skirt on the couch to rub his beard and mouth off. Then he finishes the job by drying his chin on the rug. Can't blame the boy for wanting to be clean. If ruined couches skirts or rugs are not what we want, I figure out quickly that I can wipe off his mouth for him with a napkin or paper towel. Needless to say, Chips' advanced training of his parents moves along quickly.

Our dog impresses other people we meet with his manners and gentle nature. As we take him with us wherever we can, and his behavior is noted, we constantly hear "your dog is so well behaved." I think, yeah, he's well treated – not jerked, pulled, punished or yelled at. He's asked politely or reasoned with. Of course, at our front door, he is, like most dogs, exuberant in an effort to be recognized or say hello to our guests. We don't want to suppress his natural instincts but we try to keep his jumping to a minimum. After all, don't we all want to be recognized and acknowledged? Sam and I always bend down to greet him when we come in, so he doesn't have to jump, but if others don't, the dog naturally has to go up. How else can their species reach us?

"He just wants to say hello" I tell our friends, a tolerant bunch. They usually pet him for a second –such a small thing to ask for, but that's all the greeting Chips ever needs. My friend Jane, the first to bring our dog a bag of cookies, immediately becomes his godmother.

"My dog would never behave so well," many people tell us in stores or restaurants. Of course, lots of people never take their dogs anywhere except to their front yards. So when these pets finally do go out they're naturally wild with energy. Then their guardians conclude

that their pets are not meant to leave home, and sometimes never do again.

Over time, Chips engages with hundreds of people
in outdoor restaurants, stores, the streets of Beverly
Hills, Carmel, San Francisco and all over L.A. People, especially women, just have to touch him. Chips'
expressive face, alert yet kindly, invites them. And
he's a real socialite, savoring the attention – going
right up to people who stop and pet him. Sam and I
meet dozens of Chips' contacts over the years, a few of
whom become close friends. One young man at a piz-
zeria who asks about and begins petting Chips eventually becomes a business protégé of Sam's. When the
young man marries and has his first born, a son, Sam
and I are named Godparents. Naturally, Chips is the
God-dog.

Nothing beats an appealing pooch for finding
new friends, as all dog parents can attest. People just
seem to assume that those out with their dogs are completely approachable. Facilitating these interactions is
yet one more service dogs provide us, in addition to
companionship, helping the blind, deaf, handicapped,
drug enforcement officers, the police, armed forces,
patients in hospitals. Now if I could only get Chips to
write scripts... After I had a book on married men and

the women in their lives published in the eighties, I began to get questions from women about good places to meet single men. I can think of no better place than an animal park or popular dog walking path, where there's an easy way to start a conversation. "And any guy" I tell them "who gives up his Saturday morning to make sure his dog has a good time is already a cut above the average."

Chips proceeds with *my* nighttime training. During his visits to our bed, he always scratches his neck. Of course, he has a collar there making an unimpeded pleasure impossible. I think about how it must feel to be constantly wearing a tight or even a loose ring of metal or leather around your neck, weighted with tags. Chips wears the lightest cloth collar we could find, but some dogs have thick, metal ones, which are heavy. Nonetheless, I decide early on to remove the collar at night. Not only does this provide a good scratching surface, but it gives him complete freedom while he sleeps.

In no time flat it's me doing all the neck scratching. I love the honesty of dogs who let you know exactly what they need. I wish more people did that. Following this routine, Chips becomes his most appreciative and affectionate, rolling on his back and wiggling around playfully on the bed. These little rituals we have through the years definitely make us closer. Sam also participates, scratching or rubbing Chips' tummy as he rolls. Our boy knows he can count on us to take care of these requests. After all, there are so many times when we have no choice but to disappoint him with our parting shot, "Come back soon."

And if any doubt remains about Sam's feelings for Chips they could be easily summed up by a letter I find on his desk one day.

"Dear Mr. _____

Thank you for your offer to become CEO of your company. Clearly, the salary of two million per year is more than sufficient. However, I must decline at this time. My wife and I have recently acquired a new dog. This poor fellow came from a pound, before which he was probably maltreated. We are thus spending a substantial amount of time with him until his anxieties are resolved.

My decision is in no way related to your offer or the excellent management team your corporation has in place. I feel that this indeed is an opportunity never to be matched. However, I would be pleased to serve as a consultant or join your board in exchange for access to your corporate jet in the event that Chips needs an emergency trip to see a veterinarian at U.C. Davis or wants to visit our family with us in New York. Again, thanks for the generous offer and I look forward to your early reply."

Although obviously scribblings done in jest, probably while on hold during some phone call, the letter shows his state of mind. I wonder where it will all end.

Chapter 12

I NEVER MET A
TREE I DIDN'T LIKE

*They are better than Beings, because they know and
do not tell.*

EMILY DICKINSON

"Are you somebody?" a voice calls from a van driving past me and Chips.

"Absolutely not," I assure the Midwestern woman on one of the "Homes of the Stars" tours that daily wind through the hills where we live. Taking out your dog in our neighborhood ensures such encounters while exposing you to the many canines never walked by owners. The "owners" who do walk their dogs are far outnumbered by housekeepers, housemen, dog walkers or nobody. The unluckiest of these pets are stuck in their yards all day, alone, left to cry or bark at the lucky ones that get taken out for walks. Unlike less affluent areas, dogs in Beverly Hills are not tied up because almost all the yards are totally fenced. But the guardians of these lonely guys must not realize that dogs left without walks all day are bored and miserable, becoming more aggressive or depressed as time goes by. Over the years I have seen long lived breeds die after only a few years of such solitary confinement. Also, there's always the chance they will be dognapped and sold to some horrible laboratory. These things actually happen.

And no matter how big the yard, a dog naturally wants to be with someone to go out to explore the world, sniff where other dogs have peed and pooped and hopefully run into others of his kind. They need to check out "the news." I've read that smelling the excrement or butt of another canine is not some disgusting perversion thought up to annoy "owners", but a canine way of determining the food source, something dogs once had to do when fending for themselves in the wild. Now it may only come down to Whole Foods or Pavillions. But going out walking is life! It's fun! And it involves human companionship.

I dread passing by the houses where the "prisoners" come up to the fence, desperately sticking their noses and paws through the openings and under the gates, trying to make contact with Chips. He always cries and looks at me as if to say, "Can't you do something about this?" He has seen us pick up lost dogs and get them home if they have tags, so he expects that I can help them in all circumstances. I'm frustrated that I can't. In my mind these are "the prisoners of Beverly Hills."

During the first year with Chips we keep running into Poa, the fetching blond Tibetan Terrier I've seen walking in our neighborhood. Eventually, we become friends with her guardians, who live a few blocks from us. The wife, a lovely woman and psychotherapist, invites Chips and I to come over during one of our afternoon walks. It only takes one visit, which includes a few dog cookies, to make this Chips' favorite neighborhood stop. Once inside the house he and Poa usually head straight for the huge fenced in backyard behind it. The screen door is easy for both of them to open. They run around the yard and have a great time, but Chips seems to be playing hard to get. He likes Poa; in fact he always pulls me into her driveway if we walk by the house. But after a few minutes Chips stops romping with her and seems more interested in keeping his nose to the ground, sniffing and peeing in as many places as possible. Poa usually follows him around. All in all it's a good, safe play date for both of them.

After a few visits, my new friend, Paula, and I are chatting in her kitchen when I glance out the back window and see Poa alone. I can't spot Chips, but the yard has a back area that is sunken below the rest of the property – I wouldn't see him if he was there. Something tells me to check it out. I walk all the way across the yard to that section with Chips nowhere in sight. "I'll check the gates" Paula says, heading to the side of the property. Sure enough, one of them has been left open by the gardener. I become frantic, calling "Chips come!" while running toward the open gate. Once outside I look quickly in both directions. No Chips. Then a man passing on the street asks "Are you looking for a black and white dog?

"Yes!"

"I saw him heading for the corner." He points to the corner where plenty of rush hour traffic is going both ways. Tears well in my eyes as I picture my poor boy hit by a car; I run toward the corner still yelling his name. Just then I glance back and see Chips running toward me. I can't believe my luck. In two seconds flat I grab him up in my arms. "Oh Chips, Chips, don't ever do that again," I tell him, taking him back in the yard. Smiling, I cry amidst my friend's apologies for her gardener. I'm just thrilled to have my boy back. I silently promise to check all gates myself before ever letting him off leash anywhere again.

During the following years I see many dogs running in our neighborhood for just the same reason — some gardener or pool man forgot to close a gate. Many trees are covered in posters advertising for lost dogs. In one such incident, my brother-in-law's Bichon, the one who survived the coyote attack, is again attacked, this time by a big Chow. The Bichon was being walked by the housekeeper when the larger animal, aggressive after years of isolation in a yard, got out courtesy of a careless gardener. The Bichon later died of the wounds.

During the first year walking Chips I notice that some of the housekeepers in our area are good with the dogs they walk, some aren't, and some just spend their time talking to their friends on a corner or in the small park, while the dogs stand and wait. All the while the "owners" think their pets are getting exercise. But one housekeeper really impresses me. She's marvelous with the multiple dogs she has on leash. Almost every day I see her with one or more of a half dozen different dogs in tow, all mutts, some with physical disabilities. My curiosity is peaked because this motley crew is beautifully groomed and treated. Eventually, I meet the guardian of these well cared for pets – Mrs. Peter Falk. The Falks live not far from us and have only rescued animals. I greatly admire how well they care for their six or seven, sometimes handicapped, dogs always in residence.

Chips, meanwhile, turns out to be an Olympic peeer and sniffer. If there were an event in that category, I'm sure he would take the gold. Before selecting his bathroom, he smells with such discrimination and intensity that we speculate about whether he might be a great drug sniffing candidate for the police. Of course, they won't be getting him, although if the salary were high enough...

If we try to hurry Chips' along with a tug on the leash or some words of encouragement, he looks indignantly at us, with the hauteur of the snootiest wine critic, positively insulted. "Are you actually rushing me here," I swear the expression on his face says. A toilet to a dog is a place where another has already gone. Chips takes his time in the selection process.

No matter how inconvenient the spot or how he has to balance his body on an incline or climb into brambles or plants to hit the exact right place, Chips goes for it. And he lifts his leg even if there are no supplies left in his arsenal. Unlike female dogs, who squat and pee one or two long times during a walk, the guys want to sprinkle their nectar in as many locations as possible.

Sam counts Chips' pee stops during one walk. Twenty-seven is the number that day. Though Chips lifts his leg, as male dogs do, during walks, it always amuses us that when in our yard, he merely squats like a female to relieve himself. No need to prove you're top dog in a place where you're the only one.

On one early morning walk, I'm out alone with Chips on Crescent Drive, about a half block above the legendary Beverly Hills Hotel. Another animal whizzes by across the street. I doubletake as the coyote almost flies along. Again, Chips doesn't move. He just looks at me as if to say "Terrorist?" On that same outing I see what has to be the funniest or laziest man "walking" his dog. The guy is actually driving his car, with the leash across the front seat, going out the passenger window to the dog who is trotting along on the sidewalk. The man drives as the dog walks. The obvious inherent danger of this arrangement does not seem to faze either of them.

One quirky thing Chips also does on walks is want to cross the street...for no apparent reason. I guess he's heard "The grass is always greener" thing. Neither Sam nor I see any reason to object to his crossing over, so we let him lead us. In fact, our philosophy in general is that, unless there's a good reason to say "no," Chips pretty much gets his way.

Adding to a natural inclination to cross any street is Chips' desire to greet whomever of his species happens to be there. Often in L.A. the owner or housekeeper or walker makes it clear from his or her body language and pulling their dogs away that they aren't interested in a "meet and greet." Some people and their dogs are more social, of course, and those I always let Chips say hello to.

I quickly learn to ask "Is your dog friendly?" If there's any hesitance or equivocation, I know a bite can be the potential outcome of that encounter. Although never really bitten on these walks, Chips receives a few snaps and one nip from another dog I am assured is friendly. I always keep the leash very short for these encounters unless I see both tails wagging and clear warmth on the other side. One night, while I'm in bed with a cold, Sam takes Chips out alone and is accosted by two bulldogs who pull away from the "owner". They head straight for Chips, jumping on him before Sam grabs him off the ground. Sam falls in the process, ripping his pants' and hurting his knee, but he manages to keep Chips out of harm. In case it isn't yet crystal clear, Sam has become Chips' defender sine qua non.

Interestingly enough, Beverly Hills' dogs and their people are far more likely to be unfriendly than dogs and owners in Carmel, on the central California coast, where we often visit. I try to figure out why. Was the movie and TV business responsible for the suspicious social climate? One can only speculate. If so, it has migrated down to canine relationships.

Shortly after the millennium, Beverly Hills institutes diagonal crossing in the downtown area, with the traffic lights indicating a full "walk" interval for all directions. After Chips gets used to this diagonal crossing largess, he assumes he can do it at any corner, anywhere. It takes some strong urging on my part to convince him to return to regular right angle crossing when we are somewhere else. "First we have to cross this way," I try to explain as I'm tugging him straight across. This inconsistency obviously confuses him – humans doing these strange things at some times, but not at others. From a dog's perspective, the constantly changing rules must seem like one more bizarre human foible.

Another unique habit Chips acquires – sitting suddenly while walking. At first I can't figure it out, but people need teaching too. I soon realize that if Chips picks up something in his paw, or even on top of his foot or leg – a burr, a stone, a twig or, incredibly, even a long piece of dried grass, he waits for me to remove it. How on the world did this guy make it on the street for even a day? A burr or something in the paw one can understand, but a piece of grass?! He's like the princess and the pea – the childhood story in which the princess could feel a pea under stacks of many mattresses, so sensitive were her royal sensibilities. Well, Chips was no doubt the prince analogue of that girl. It takes a lot of control not to laugh at the way he just sits and waits to be serviced, secure in the confidence that mom or dad will remove the offending vegetation. If it really is a stone or burr, he simply lifts his paw to make things easier. But even the innocuous piece of dried grass bothers him. After braving life on the streets and in the pound, he's quickly become a Beverly Hills wuss.

One day, out walking, Sam, Chips and I see a Dachshund, by himself, crossing the street. Chips knows that we've returned to their homes several dogs who've gotten out of yards. We walk over to the dog and I read his tag. It has his name, "Henry," and a phone number, but no address. I always wonder what people are thinking when they do that. How can anyone bring a dog back home if they don't know where he lives? Sometimes there's no one home or there's someone who doesn't answer the phone. If you know the location, at least you can learn whether the dog has traveled far or near.

A friend of ours once picked up a Labrador Retriever in the hills. He was afraid the dog would be run over in the streets with no sidewalks. There was a phone number but no address on the dog's tag. They took the dog to their house. After a few hours, my friend reached the "owner" – the dog had in fact been in front of his own house where he'd gone out the doggy door to pick up the newspaper. Had my friend known the address, she would have rung the bell.

When we walk over to the Dachshund, I say to Sam, "Take off your belt and we can make a leash." Sam does, and I put one end through the dog's collar and the belt buckle, then hold the other end. "Let's try leading him back in the direction he came from. Maybe he'll show us his house." Chips goes right to Henry and walks slightly ahead of him, seeming to understand the game plan. Sure enough, Henry trots right up the front path of a nearby house. We ring and knock. No answer. Chips paws the door. We call the number on the tag, get a machine and leave a message. I decide to go around the back with Henry just in case there are people in the yard or a door has been left ajar. No one there.

I really don't know why I try the closed back door, but to my astonishment it's open. Henry walks right into the kitchen of this house like he owns the place. I close the door and rejoin Sam on the sidewalk. "Would you believe the door was unlocked? Who in Beverly Hills would do this?" Though Henry seemed right at home, it could possibly be the wrong house. What if the people come home and find a strange dog there?

"Maybe the people were robbed and the thieves left the door unlocked." As we're discussing this, Chips starts to whine. We turn around to see what he's staring at. It's Henry again! The Dachshund walks toward us. How in the world did he get out of a closed door? Chips leads us to the back while we carry Henry. We want to see if the door has blown open. No. It's closed like I'd left it. The gate to the yard is open, but I'd put Henry in the house. Walking to the other side of the home, I spot two French doors wide open. Not unlocked, but standing open. Now a robbery seemed a surer thing. We place Henry back inside, close all the doors and call the Beverly Hills Police. As reputed, they arrive fast - - their usual three minutes. We relate Henry's story. The police look at us with a bit of skepticism. "And who are you?" They take our names and address. Finally, they seemed convinced that we live in the neighborhood, and tell us we can leave; they'll go through the house. We ask that they call us if they intend to take the dog out of there and need somewhere to drop him. We don't want another dog going to the pound.

Only after two days do we discover what actually happened. A man calls to tell us that he is the guardian and had been out of town when he got away. His wife had rushed from the house without locking the doors, which their sons actually left open. When she returned she never called our number. We were surprised about how casual the whole thing seemed to them. At least two other times, we spot Henry alone on the street near their home. Living in Beverly Hills is no assurance of a dog being well cared for.

Chapter 13

A TAIL OF TWO CITIES

The dog succeeds in piercing, in order to draw closer to us, the partitions, ever elsewhere impermeable, that separate the species!"

MAETERLINCK

We decide to drive to Carmel, six hours north of L.A., to visit Sam's business partner and his wife. These friends have a house on a bluff over the ocean in Carmel Highlands. It's the first glimpse of the ocean that Chips ever had. (If he'd never even seen stairs it was unlikely that he went too many places before we found him.) The water there surges wildly, slamming against the rocks as gulls and all manner of birds fly in and out of the inlets and rocks. Sometimes otters and dolphins swim by, the otters each with a rock under his or her flipper to crack clams or other shellfish. I take Chips to the edge of the bluff where he sits transfixed, almost hypnotized. It's the longest time I've ever seen him watch anything. I sense the deep peace and fascination that Chips feels.

The ocean never stops fascinating our boy. The first time Chips actually goes near the water himself, on the leash-free beach in Carmel, he barks at the ocean every time a wave breaks. He never outgrows barking at the ocean like that, and we've never seen another dog do it. While he runs furiously along the water's edge, Chips keeps checking to see if I'm close by. I stay as near as I can, concerned lest he meet a four legged bully. I've heard about the rare biting incident, and our dog was by now a mama's boy for sure.

Carmel is dog heaven. Almost all the stores have treats for them. Even the bank teller has a stash of cookies, two of which she gives Chips. In fact the majority of stores and offices find the business owners' and some of the workers' dogs with them during the day. Chips easily becomes convinced that all cashiers have cookies, a potential source of pleasure he was just discovering. In short order, instead of waiting to be offered a treat, Chips tries leading me into stores, then marches right up to the cashier's desk with his irresistible face, raises his paw, offering to shake hands, which he knows usually does the trick. Rarely disappointed, he gets so used to this routine, that when we return to Los Angeles he continues to go up to every cashier's desk in every store and raise his paw, certain a cookie will follow his heartfelt offer. But all places are not Carmel.

When, back in L.A., if no treat is forthcoming, Chips turns, looks at me, as if to say, "What'd I do wrong?"

"I'm sorry," some of the cashiers tell him.

All I can say to him is "...no cookie." This he understands but certainly doesn't like. "Such are life's ups and downs," I explain. One store in Beverly Hills is Chips' paws down favorite. He drags me to Francis Orr on Camden Drive every time we're even blocks away. You'd think they were selling lamb-chops the way he wants to go there, but it's actually a dog named Ozzie, a gorgeous Australian Shepherd, who's the lure. Ozzie "works" there. Chips just likes this dog, can't wait to see him. Now Ozzie is bigger and more rambunctious than Chips, but my little guy loves to visit his friend. Sometimes Ozzie is not there but out for a walk or off for the day with his guardian. Chips darts in and out of the aisles searching. "No Ozzie,"

I tell Chips when his friend's not there. Afterwards, he heads to the cashier's desk for a cookie. He almost always gets it, which makes the trip not a total loss.

Four years after Chips comes to live with us we rent a small, four room house in Carmel for the month of September, always the hottest one in L.A. On September 11th 2001, I awaken to the sound of distant voices. I glance at the clock; it reads six forty-five. Sam is not in bed. Neither is Chips. Very strange. Who are the voices, I wonder. Sleepily, I wander into the living room to find Sam standing in front of the only TV in the house, an old one inside a cabinet. I see planes crashing into buildings on the screen. "Why are you watching a disaster movie at this hour," I ask.

"It's not a movie. This is happening right now. Julie called me to turn on the TV." I cannot fathom what Sam means. His younger sister had apparently called his cell phone to alert him. Chips is also there wondering I suppose why his sleep was interrupted.

"Are you telling me that in New York a plane..."

"Two planes just crashed into the World Trade Center."

"Oh, my God. Oh God. This has to be Osama Bin Laden. Didn't I tell you they'd be back after that blind sheik tried to blow it up in '93?"

"That's right."

"Wait. That's where Marion works." My eyes begin to tear. My closest friend, whose first name is the same as mine, works right around there. "I think it's the twin towers." I dial my friend's office but all the phone lines to New York are naturally jammed. "I've got to call her mother." I go to the phone and dial my friend's mother in Fort Lauderdale. As the phone rings I realize that she might not know what's happening. It's three hours later in the East. Maybe she's out or her television isn't on. After a few rings, the answering machine kicks on. I try to swallow my tears. "Hi, Beverly. It's the other Marion. Would you please call me as soon as you have a moment." She knows my voice and I try not to alarm her in the message, but my voice is impossible to control. Next I dial my family members, most of whom still live in New York. The lines of course are still jammed.

I call my mother also living in Fort Lauderdale. She's watching TV. "I haven't been able to reach the rest of the family either," she says. Like almost every other American, Sam and I stay glued in horror to the TV, both standing in front of the small screen. Chips looks at us quizzically, sensing something is very wrong.

About twenty minutes later, my friend's mother calls back. I pick up the phone. "Hello?"

"She's all right!" Beverly's voice announces in relief. "I just spoke to her – she got out and called me on her cell."

"Was she in the World Trade Center?"

"No. That's what I thought, but she's in the World Financial Center." My friend worked for Merrill Lynch in the building nearby. We both cry on the phone. In order to watch the unfolding events I postpone Chips' morning walk, putting him in the small yard behind the house. Later on, walking him on the path above the beach, I see very few people out. By the next day, there are tables set up in town where American flag pins are being sold and money collected for the New York firemen and rescue workers. And I'm then able to reach my family in New York. Also, Marion tells me about the horrors she has seen following the crash.

"It was the worst day of my life." Knowing what she'd seen and been through, I believe her. Between constantly watching the news, visiting a few friends in Carmel and taking long walks in the area, the four weeks there fly by and we begin discussing another possible visit in late November.

"How about a week here for our anniversary," Sam suggests.

"Great idea. I guess we could stay at the Cypress Inn." That's a well located hotel once owned by Doris Day, which allows dogs. Several other establishments do also.

"It's one possibility." But we know that at the hotel you aren't allowed to leave the dog alone in the room when you go out. Staying there would require being outside with the dog whenever we went out or leaving him in the car at the end of November. It could be cold. "Or we could rent someplace." Just as we're discussing this, we pass, on a lovely street near the beach, a typical new Carmel house, small but charming in the English country manner. It had a "For Rent" sign out front.

"You think they'd take a dog?"

"Probably not, but we could ask" Sam says. I ring the bell. A young man of about twenty answers. "We'd like to inquire about renting your beautiful house for a week at the end of November.

"Sure."

"What is the price?"

"A thousand a week." That was about the going rate. "Would you like to see it?"

We walk through this recently built, beautifully done cottage with two bedrooms, wood floors, a miniscule den, living room cum dining room, good sized kitchen and two baths.

"It's absolutely lovely."

"O.k., but we don't take dogs," he says glancing down at Chips.

"Oh, he's never had an accident in all the time we've had him. And he doesn't chew on anything but food. Honest," I say raising my right hand. Sam backs me up at this point.

"I'm sorry, but my parents told me 'no dogs'."

"We'd be happy to leave a substantial deposit against damages," Sam chimes in.

"Look at him," I say smiling. Does he look like he could do any harm?"

"I just don't know. He's very cute. I guess I could talk to my dad." The idea at least wasn't dismissed. Sam writes down our name and phone number.

"In case you change your minds," Sam says handing him the paper. The next day we receive a call saying that we could have the house with a five hundred dollar deposit against damages from the dog. We aren't concerned because Chips' toilet habits and docile ways are totally reliable. We book the house for the week we want.

A few days before our anniversary the three of us drive up to Carmel. Between lunch and our pit stops it's about a six and a half hour trip. Chips always starts out in his favorite position – standing back legs on the back seat and front legs balanced on the compartment between the front seats, his head between ours. We let him do this so that he can better see the passing scenery, but as soon as we get on a freeway, we tell him to "go in the back" so as to prevent him falling when we use the brakes. By now using the seatbelt has become impossible – he just gets totally tangled up in it.

In Carmel, as per instructions, we pick up the key from a neighbor, carry in our luggage and Chips' bed, then go upstairs to the bedroom.

"Let's take him out for a walk before we unpack," I suggest.

"All right. You want to go for a walk?" Sam asks Chips. He is standing on the white carpet in the bedroom, which has the only carpet in the house. He begins to heave, as in carsick. I'd seen him do this before. "Oh no!" I virtually leap over to him, but it's too late. He barfs some yellow liquid I recognize as bile. "I guess he got carsick," I announce.

"The only carpet in the house," Sam laments. "You have your stuff?" My husband refers to a cleanser designed to clean up substances emitted from either end of a dog or cat.

"Of course." It usually works quite well. I blot up what I can with paper towels, pour on the stuff and allow it to set while we go for a walk. I follow the bottle's cleaning instructions when we return. It gets out most of the stain, but some discoloration remains – which, of course, looks as bad as possible on white carpeting.

The next evening we have dinner with Sam's partner, Wally, and his wife, Lu. We tell them about the carpet problem. "I have just what you need" Lu says. "This stuff gets out anything. It's great." She pours a little into a jar and gives it to us. I'm determined to fix the damage I had promised would never happen.

When we reach home I immediately go to work on the spot again. It's pretty wet but still looks discolored. "Maybe by tomorrow it'll all dry up fine," Sam says encouragingly. We all go to sleep. The next day we awake to see no improvement in the stain. When I think of the assurances we'd given the young man I feel just awful, as if I'd done it myself. There's also the five hundred dollars.

"We better call a carpet cleaner," Sam suggests. We get out the yellow pages and make an appointment. One hundred dollars later, after the cleaner's visit, we receive the bad news.

"If you'd just used the first thing, we could have fixed it," the man says. "But that second liquid I'm afraid set the stain permanently." Oh no. I saw our now six hundred dollars and maybe more taking permanent leave of us.

Despite the accident we all had a splendid week. Chips even made the local Carmel newspaper – "The Pine Cone." In a column entitled "Sandy Claws," one dog is featured with his photo and bio each week. Since Chips happened to be at the right time and place (isn't that always the way with stardom?) he runs into the woman who finds her subjects on the walking path above the beach. This week, Chips lucks out. He appears with a photo and the headline "From Beverly Hills Hotspots to Carmel Beach." Sam manages to take about a dozen copies back with us to L.A. Afterwards, Carmel friends, thinking we might have missed it, send an additional six copies. So, we have a large collection of Chips' clippings to send to family and friends in L.A. Would Sam send it to former business associates, I wonder. Should we dispense the clippings as prizes at our next dinner party?

Celebrity didn't seem to change our boy one iota. And the carpet, according to our landlord, cost exactly five hundred dollars to replace. I told Chips "you're wonderful, but expensive," the thousand dollar week having turned into a sixteen hundred dollar one. He seemed unconcerned as we walked away from his last run on the beach.

Carmel's leash-free beach is as close to paradise as any dog can find. Unfortunately, Chips' days of running there are few. Sometimes, in trying to do everything right, we stumble.

Chapter 14

THE COST OF A
BEAUTIFUL SMILE

*What is it makes us more than dust? My trust in
him, in me his trust.*

SIGFRIED SASSOON

At some point during Chips' first year with us we
learn that humans are supposed to brush their dogs'
teeth. Are they kidding? But just like us, they can
develop dental problems from plaque build-up which,
if neglected, terminates in gum disease or the loss of
teeth. I know that many people will think, "Come on,
dogs in the wild never brushed their teeth." But they
also didn't live as long as dogs protected by humans
and treated medically, so their teeth didn't need

to last too long. No doubt who was going to do this job! Though Sam is one of those people who actually brushes his teeth after every meal, and has them cleaned three to four times a year, he would not sign up for the canine oral hygiene brigade.

Dutifully, I buy the toothbrush and chicken flavored toothpaste. I smear the toothpaste on the wet brush and let Chips sniff it. His tongue immediately shoots out. "Just a minute there." I hold back the toothpaste until I raise his lip and try brushing his teeth. All I manage to get are the two big front ones on either side.

I soon discover that Chips is a clencher, and a master at keeping his teeth out of reach. In between sneaking his tongue out for the toothpaste, he clamps his mouth shut so tight that no amount of prying would budge the teeth apart. The outside of the side teeth are a possibility, but anything else, a losing struggle. I try repeatedly to pry those teeth open with my thumb and then the toothbrush, but fail miserably. I feel incompetent, a bad mom whose charge would end up with rotten teeth. Chips didn't see it that way – he loves licking the chicken toothpaste off his mouth where it all eventually winds up, but, try as I might, time and again, I keep failing.

I then buy green, toothbrush-shaped dog treats which are supposed to help clean the dogs' teeth as they eat them. Chips can't get enough of these new things, but a moment after they're consumed, out they come again partially digested and usually on our rugs. The cleaning liquid helps but the results are far from perfect. These new treats go in the garbage. Although Chips never has an accident from his posterior end, the evidence of numerous vomiting incidents remains on our rugs over the years. In addition to Chips' other little problems, he naturally has a sensitive stomach.

Another call to Nancy, the woman who saved Chips from the pound. "Use the non-anesthetic teeth cleaner," she tells me. I discover that Nancy pays a woman to come over and clean her dogs' teeth without anesthesia. The vets, I knew, did the cleaning *with* anesthesia. Nancy's own seven rescue dogs all have their teeth cleaned regularly. Obviously, it's best to avoid anesthesia when possible, but I intuitively feel that Chips would not be a willing patient. I hesitantly call the doggy dental hygienist.

Cindy comes over with her kit. "I doubt that Chips will cooperate with our cleaning plans." I tell her.

"I've only met one dog in my life whose teeth I could not clean." You're about to meet your second,

I think. Cindy takes Chips into the dining room and sits down on the floor with him. No luck. After one or two tries she comes back. "It would be better if I took him around the side of the house where he can't see you." I reluctantly agree. After about thirty minutes she comes back with Chips, whose whole mouth area is wet. "It went well," she assures me. "He has a lot of plaque. The best thing is to do this cleaning every month so it won't build up too much."

"I only do my own teeth every six months."

"But your teeth are cleaned more thoroughly. With the dogs we have to do a little at a time."

"I'll think about it." I could see my remaining work time dwindling away. Another call to Nancy.

"Yes, I do my own dogs once a month because it really does work better. If you bring Chips over here it won't cost much because she comes here anyway," she tells me. Cost is not the issue – it's only about twenty dollars. But the time involved just seems like a big commitment. But, hey, I don't want Chips' teeth to fall out. Persistently, I still try the toothbrush and chicken toothpaste. No great luck. After our anniversary trip to Carmel and my continued failure to brush Chips' choppers myself, I decide to give the professional cleaner a chance. Nancy lives only a few blocks from us, so it won't be too long a process.

The owner of that business, Cindy, injures her knee a few weeks later and can't clean Chips' teeth again. But Vicky, who works for her, takes over. I peek over the fence into an area outside Nancy's house to make sure all is well while Vicky, a seemingly competent woman, works on Chips' teeth. She has him between her legs, his back to her, holds his lip up with one hand and wields the instrument with the other. After about five months of this routine, Chips and I are confronted by Vicky and her sister, a new gal she's training. I assume that Vicky will just repeat her usual procedure to demonstrate the technique. But when I look over the fence, I see Chips' head being held tilted too far back, in an unnatural position. I immediately go to the area and ask "What are you doing?" Then I notice that she has a round stick holding open my dog's mouth. "What are you doing," I repeat.

The sister replies, "Your dog is very spoiled." My translation – "I have to strong arm your animal because I don't know what I'm doing."

"Give him to me," I immediately say, taking out my wallet to pay her.

"That's o.k.," Vicky says. "I'm sorry."

At least she recognizes that they are not handling Chips correctly. I leave at once. When I get him home, Chips isn't walking right. He moves slowly, his movements awkward. When I try to pick him up, he screams. I call the vet, who tells us to come right over. Dr. Olds, an outstanding orthopedic surgeon, examines Chips. "He seems to have a problem with his neck." I tell him about the teeth cleaning. "Why don't you try some acupuncture before resorting to anything more drastic?"

I am pleasantly surprised and impressed that a traditional vet would recommend someone in another area of veterinary medicine. Before we leave we tell him that Chips did not drink any water since he came back and seems dehydrated. One of the women vets there gives him some hydration under the skin with a small needle inserted into the back. This doesn't seem to bother him.

The holistic vet/acupuncturist Dr. Olds recommended is about forty-five minutes away. We wonder how Chips, who doesn't like people other than us handling him, would allow someone new to put in multiple needles. I hold him while the acupuncturist places the needles in. No big problem. But keeping him still for twenty minutes while they do their work is nearly impossible. Chips squirms and wants to get off the table. Sam and I just stroke him, and I sing a couple of choruses of "Shine On Harvest Moon," which may be the reason that Chips is so anxious to leave. As I reach the last "Snow time aint no time to sit outdoors and spoon" the vet comes back to remove the needles.

Immediately after having the needles removed, Chips seems to be moving with more ease. Unfortunately, this doesn't last. A few hours later, his condition worsens. We call Dr. Olds the next day. "Chips can't even lie down comfortably, and is standing strangely, in one spot. If I try to pick him up, he yelps. Something is very wrong."

The doctor recommends an immediate MRI to see what's actually going on. An x-ray could not tell the whole story. So we go, as instructed, to a canine MRI facility (who knew?), which looks exactly like a normal radiology office. Actually, the woman who does the procedure is a radiologist working at UCLA Medical Center in the afternoons. Sam and I nervously carry Chips, in his bed, into the facility. There's no other way we can lift him without him yelping. He isn't doing well. The radiologist gives him a tranquilizing shot and puts in a shunt for the catheter to anaesthetize him. The MRI takes a long time, almost two hours.

I talk to the receptionist repeatedly and am told that the machine has to go slowly over his upper body with its many small disks, bones and soft tissue. I know the cost of this would have been impossible for many people to handle. Sam and I talk about what happens to dogs like Chips when someone who can't afford this care is his "owner".

"Obviously, such dogs are put down every day." We thank God that we are in a position to help Chips this way. When we adopted him, I suggested getting pet medical insurance. Sam wasn't that keen on it, but we did a little research. When we received the initial policy information it was vague about what specifically was covered. I tried to pin down the information, but was told that they would let us know if a procedure or illness was covered as we went along. We both thought that answer was ridiculous and probably indicated that, like many HMOs, they'd simply turn down claims. We didn't get it, but when we paid the MRI bill we regretted the decision. That, however, is our least concern at the moment.

After what seems forever, the doctor calls us in to view the results of the MRI. "Chips clearly has a shattered neck disk," she says, pointing to an area on the MRI. Obviously that happened during the teeth cleaning with his head pulled so far back. "I left the catheter in him for easier access. You should probably do immediate surgery with Dr. Olds." We know he's the best orthopedic surgeon around. Our pathetic little guy, just coming out of the anesthetic, looks confused and still in pain. We agree to the radiologist calling the surgeon, only blocks away. "He wants you to come right over."

Sam has a tear in his eye as we carry Chips' out to the car. I hold my boy in the back seat while Sam drives very slowly, trying to avoid potholes, to Dr. Olds' office. After the surgeon studies the film he explains, "The pieces of shattered disk need to be removed from Chips' neck. Then the surrounding disks can fuse. They should fuse and he could fully recover," he says.

I notice that he says "could" not "will." Obviously we have no choice. Chips is in pain and can't walk. Once again, we leave our beloved pet for surgery. After Sam and I are assured by Dr. Olds that Chips will be given all appropriate post-operative pain killers, we're told to call later that day. Depressed, we drive home, realizing how profoundly Chips has affected our relationship, making us move in unison, become even closer, though sometimes disagreeing about what's best for him. Sam always leans toward physical safety, caution, protection. I definitely want him to have more joy, impulse satisfaction, emotional highs. Chips reflects our natural inclinations and different personalities. "You think he'll make it?" I ask Sam. My husband looks at me with so much sadness, I'm sorry I asked.

At the end of the day we get a phone call from the Brentwood Pet Clinic. "Chips is doing well," a woman tells us. I start breathing again. It's the first night that we will spend with him away from home. Seeing his empty bed is too depressing to do anything but go to sleep early, hoping the night will quickly disappear. Sam holds my hand in the dark while we wonder if Chips will forgive us for leaving him alone in a strange place to again have violence done to his small body. "I told you he was a poor little guy," Sam whispers as we fall asleep.

The next day we visit the veterinary clinic to find Chips in a cage with an intravenous line in his leg. His throat had been cut where the doctor went in from the front to remove the pieces of shattered disc in his neck. We stroke him in the cage, but, in his drug induced state, he barely raises his head to look at us. No anger shows in his expression, but a resignation that this is destiny – more suffering in a cage. I'm not saying that he actually contemplated fate or destiny, but that he knew that submission was the only course available to him.

"Chips might go home later today if he continues doing well" Dr. Olds says. It's Friday, closing time, when they bring us our boy, his throat lightly bandaged with a gauze over the stitches. A morphine patch hugs his middle; we're given a bottle of pain pills to administer when he cries. We'd brought his bed in to carry him to the car. I again sit in the back with him, stroking his head while Sam drives as carefully as possible to our house.

That night Chips eats a little food. We both carry him upstairs in his bed, but get little sleep as we keep checking on him. By the next day, he begins to whimper. I take out a pain pill but know by now that Chips is not the kind of dog to take pills by themselves. I put the small white disk into a lump of almond butter, which he normally loves, but won't take. Next, I try cream cheese. Success!

Sam and I are scheduled to go to a fiftieth birthday party of a dear friend in Palo Alto that evening. Aunt Berta originally planned to stay with Chips. But that was before the surgery. Now there can be no question about leaving him without Sam or me. "I don't want to leave," he says. But we finally agree that it would be better if one of us shows up at the party rather than neither of us. Sam very reluctantly agrees to fly there because Chips would be more upset if I left him.

Before the next pain pill is due, I try to get Chips to eat something, but he won't. I know that I'll have to stick the pill in something, but he isn't taking any food. Neither the doctor nor we had thought of the fact that when a dog is in pain, he won't eat. I have a friend pick up some bacon and chicken livers, things that I know are irresistible to dogs. They are to dogs not in pain, but after the morphine patch wears out, Chips simply stops eating and drinking. He'll take absolutely nothing. No food, no pain pill. I can't force his mouth open, shove the pill down his throat and stroke it because it's been cut and bandaged.

Being late Saturday, our vet's unreachable. There's nothing worse than seeing a helpless creature you love suffering, and being unable to do anything about it. Chips' pain became mine. My feeling of impotence would make that night one of the worst of my life.

Sam has just arrived at the birthday party up North when he calls. I try not to alarm him, but can't hide the reality of the moment. "I wish I were there to help.

I'm ready to turn around and get back on the next plane, but there aren't any flying back to L.A. for several hours."

"I'm still trying to get him to eat. Please call me from dinner." I get on the floor to stroke Chips, and begin singing softly to him. He falls asleep for a while. When he awakes, his whimpering begins again. I try all the food with the pain pills again. No luck. An emergency clinic is about twenty-five minutes away, but I can't even get Chips in the car myself. He needs very careful handling, and someone has to stabilize him while riding over the rough streets. I call a few friends in the area. No one is home. Saturday night – my boy in pain and absolutely nothing I can do about it.

I phone Sam, who can't enjoy the dinner while worrying about Chips. He's booked on the next plane back. My continuing efforts at medicating fail. "I'm sorry," I tell Chips. Knowing I'm the responsible party and that this creature depends on me for the pain relief he isn't getting induces the worst guilt I've ever had.

Mercifully, Sam arrives home about eleven thirty. We immediately drive Chips to the emergency clinic and tell them, "Please give him a morphine shot and a new patch." Five minutes later, they return a quiet bundle of black and white fur. The now calm Chips lies in the dog bed on the back seat. After we reach home, he actually eats a bit of chicken. Finally, at a quarter to two, we all go to sleep.

The following day, Sunday, is somewhat better, but by the evening, Chips stops eating and drinking again. I call the emergency clinic. "That morphine patch should be working until Monday morning," the woman tells me. Chips doesn't cry much, but still will not eat. Neither Sam nor I sleep that night. On Monday morning, we're the first people at the vet.

"You two look terrible," Dr. Olds says. We tell him what a weekend it's been, and he seems surprised that Chips had not been able to take any of the pain pills. He wants us to leave Chips with him to receive intravenous pain medication. "You guys get some rest." Exactly what we do. Later that day, we visit Chips, now resting peacefully. "Why don't you leave him here on the intravenous pain medication for a couple of nights" Dr. Olds suggests. We follow his suggestion. The worst seems to be over. By the time we take Chips back home, he is doing better. One of us stays with him all the time for the next few days. Of course we're not out of the woods. Nothing ever goes that easy for us.

While grateful for Chips' recuperation, I notice, a few days post operation, that an area on his back shows a sore. Dr. Olds gets another visit. "It's infected, probably from a hair that might have gotten trapped by the needle when he got the hydration under his skin." That took place before the surgery decision had even been made. Dr. Olds gives us a local antibiotic for the sore and puts a small tee shirt on Chips so that he won't lick the spot. Chips comes back out in a little boy's green striped tee shirt, tied in a knot at the top.

"You look quite fetching" I tell him. Nonetheless, the sore still bleeds periodically. We watch this new problem, apply the antibiotic, and Dr. Olds keeps checking its progress. Although improving, it's slow going. After a few weeks Dr. Olds suggests "you guys might go crazy waiting for this sore to heal."

"You know your customers."

"If I cut it out and stitch it, the healing will be much faster." We agree to yet another procedure. Chips gets hauled away again, but goes home with us that same day.

From the time of the neck surgery forward, Chips must wear a harness for walks, so that he won't be pulled by the neck. Probably the best idea for all dogs who are not big or difficult to handle. It also leads to far less injury and discomfort. Gradually, our boy recovers from all these traumas, but Sam now takes to calling him "poor little guy," again. I frequently find the two of them on the floor together, Sam looking into Chips' eyes and petting him. No doubt any more that Sam has taken possession of this dog in his soul. But no matter how much he does for our dog, or how he expresses his affection, Sam always gets the short end of the stick. I feel bad about it. If Sam's blocking Chips' view of me, the dog looks around or over him, sometimes even moving away to improve his view. "He doesn't like me," Sam insists.

"Of course he does. It's probably just a male female thing." I remind Sam that Daisy had been much more his dog than his former wife's. "Also, I'm the one who always feeds him, a definite advantage." As the latest medical crisis recedes, I try contacting the non-anesthetic teeth cleaning service to tell them what's occurred so they won't let this happen to other dogs. I ask to speak to Cindy, the owner of the business.

"She's not here, but you can leave a message." I do so repeatedly, but never receive a return call. After another try, I relate to the assistant the incident and am told "our employees are not trained to work that way." Apparently, Vicky's sister, who has done this harm to Chips, was very distraught at the time, as their third sister had been killed two weeks prior to this incident. Though a terrible tragedy, it in no way ameliorates the harm done to our dog. And Chips' days on the beach are over.

"Running on the soft sand would put too much strain on the neck while the vertebrae are fusing," Dr. Olds tells us. I never do reach Cindy. No matter how many messages I leave, she will not call back. Obviously she doesn't want to hear what I have to say. Perhaps it's the litigious climate in L.A. I'm not thinking lawsuit, which would do nothing to undo Chips' suffering, nor am I sure I could actually prove in a court of law what I know to be true. All I want is to talk to her, but since she never has the courtesy to call back, I can only warn my pet owning friends not to take a chance with such services. They are totally unregulated as of this moment.

Many people in animal service businesses are poorly paid folks with little or no formal training as to how to properly do their jobs. There are, of course, some fine people doing this work, but only some. After all these problems, Sam and I become extremely cautious about whom, if anyone, we ever turn our boy over to. Any future teeth cleaning would be done by our vet, under anesthesia, but I never give up on the possibility of brushing Chips' teeth myself. To encourage this habit, I bring him to my dentist's office every time I have my own teeth cleaned, so that he can see it's something quite normal to open one's mouth and have others fool around in there. At the very least I hope he'll learn to use the bowl if he wants to spit.

Lucky for me, our dentist is a dog loving soul who, along with his staff, always welcomes Chips to watch my teeth being worked on. And the waiting room fascinates him – a wonderful tank of fish rests in his reach if he just stands on his hind legs. Upon entering, he immediately gets up and puts his paws on the tank.

The first time he watches my teeth cleaning, Chips looks concerned when I open my mouth and someone puts instruments into it. He moves closer, placing his paws up on the dental chair to better see. But after a few moments he just curls up in front of it to monitor things. Despite these fine examples of harmless dental procedures, Chips' stubbornness with regard to his own brushing remains firm. He will not open his mouth except to eat, pant or play around. His talent for capturing his chicken toothpaste far exceeds my ability to get the brush in an effective position for brushing. For the moment, less than perfect teeth will have to do.

Chapter 15

DOG DAYS OF SUMMER, FALL, WINTER AND SPRING

*I would have no pleasure living in
a world where dogs did not exist.*

SCHOPENHAUER

While I'm busy finishing my script, Chips' allergies get worse. He's in my office all day, intermittently
scratching and biting. The script re-write notwith-
standing, his problems cannot be ignored. O.K. early
on, we changed Chips' kibble to one with no corn. We
don't hear any complaints from him, so we assume it's
o.k. But nothing that simple ever works for us. His
itchy paws and general scratching and biting drive us

crazy. Antihistamines aren't doing it either. Maybe he's allergic to something else. I hope it isn't us.

I scurry out to buy several books on natural medicine for dogs. They indicate that many of the allergy problems are due to commercial dog food. The books describe the crap that goes into most pet foods – the by-products and animal parts they'd normally throw away for humans. An inveterate label reader, I haven't given Chips any foods containing "by-products." Before the invention of commercial pet food, people fed dogs the same thing the family ate, usually scraps from the table. That wasn't good for them either, but at least it was real food.

We know that kibble is important for Chips' teeth, especially because he doesn't go in for the brushing. I look for the best brand of kibble I can find, where the first ingredients are what we'd eat ourselves, followed by nothing that isn't recognizable as genuine food. To this base, I add some chicken or meat, the same grade we would eat, and vegetables. Of course, Chips prefers the human food to the kibble. I cook up batches of various proteins with vegetables and brown rice, divide it into plastic bags and keep them in the freezer for him. But no matter what we feed this little guy, the itching and scratching pretty much continue. The

very first neighborhood vet we'd gone to once gave
Chips a cortisone shot to stop his itching. Of course,
no one time treatment works for long. And steroids,
we know, should be avoided when at all possible. The
object is to find a more natural solution.

Dr. Olds' partner, Dr. Martin, an outstanding
internist, recommends we see a dermatologist. One
practices in Marina del Rey, about forty minutes away.
We take Chips to this veterinary specialist, who I find
a bit cold. O.K. I tell myself, so he's not Mr. Personality. You don't have to marry the guy, just get him
to fix the scratching and biting. But since he doesn't
handle Chips all that gently, our boy pays him in kind
by snapping at him, which immediately earns him a
muzzle. The doctor wants to do scratch testing to see
what he's allergic to. We hope to find a solution that
doesn't involve putting Chips through shaving part of
his hair off, followed by scratch tests. I've had those
myself. Before subjecting him to all that, we stop next
at a holistic vet.

The three of us like this doctor, thorough and
intelligent, a lot better. He explains all about dog
allergies, and reinforces our feeling that steroids are
definitely not the way to go. He recommends administering to Chips some natural herbs in liquid form

from droppers. "He's not very cooperative when it comes to opening his mouth for medicine," I explain.

"Put the drops in his water."

"What do they taste like?"

"They're tasteless, like vodka." That would surprise all the vodka drinkers I know. We hope that Chips is willing to down some of the Russian staple without requiring any caviar to go with it. After the way we've treated him, who knows what he expects? The amount of liquid to be consumed is significant, involving several droppersful each day. Chips doesn't normally drink a lot of water, and tends to drink even less when I put this stuff in it. I stand next to his dish. "I guess vodka is not your beverage of choice."

"Don't think of adding these liquids to food," the Doctor has warned. "The potency would be too dissipated." So we can hope he drinks it, force it down or forget it. Soon it becomes obvious that forgetting it remains our only option.

The continued efforts to stop Chips' scratching and biting naturally includes flea prevention. Any responsible pet parent knows that once a month, you're supposed to use the flea prevention products, the latest incarnation being a liquid that is placed between the shoulders of the dog. Most people use one of two popular brands on the market for protection. Naturally, that method would prove too easy for us. Chips goes nuts the first time we use it, running around and rubbing his body on the floor and the sides of any piece of furniture with cloth hanging down. Then he hides. I see that his skin looks a little red where we put the liquid. Clearly he's having a bad reaction or an allergic one to the medication.

"Try the competitive brand," Dr. Martin suggests. "And divide it into two or three spots instead of one." The following month, we do as told, but Chips' reaction is the same. Years later a magazine article comes out that says some dogs have had irritations or burns from these products. Chips is clearly one of those. By now, we'd been in touch with Sam's partner's son, a large animal vet in Northern California, who's married to another vet. The couple recommends a new dermatologist they know in Los Angeles, one they'd gone to school with at UC Davis, a top veterinary institution.

Chips arrives at Dr. Werner's office with the same enthusiasm he shows for all vets – none. He displays a nervous interest in all the animals there, very friendly toward everyone, but cooperative only to the point where someone wants to actually do something to him. He prefers no examining, injecting, manipulating or otherwise appropriating of his body. How could we fault him?

We enter the waiting room, containing far fewer patients than in a regular veterinary practice. A green parrot on a perch, who lives there, immediately captures Chips' interest. In going over to meet him we're warned by the receptionist, "He's not friendly." So, at my urging, Chips turns his attention to the fish tank nearby, which he paws as the fish swim by.

After a few minutes, Dr. Werner welcomes us into his office and immediately gets down on the floor to pet Chips. Our boy maintains his usual friendly demeanor as Sam and I look at one another, relieved that the vet has a rapport with our dog who's on high alert at all vets' offices. He examines Chips' paws, looks through his hair at the skin, which he pronounces "not bad compared to many other dogs who already have hotspots, skin sores, and more advanced conditions." Of course, we're much too anxious and neurotic to let Chips get to that point before attempting to resolve the problem.

Dr. Werner suggests that we try a pill, a prescription antihistamine with a little prednisone in it. Prednisone is a steroid, but he assures us "The dose isn't large enough to be harmful, and you can discontinue it after a couple of weeks. "But to really know what's going on with Chips you need allergy testing." Same story as the first dermatologist. There isn't a food allergy test, but there is one for plants. "To test for food allergies, you can only provide a single food diet, then add in one food at a time, to see what the reaction is."

The doctor suggests for Chips' paws, his worst problem, washing them whenever he comes in from outside, or at least wiping them off with a wet cloth or Babywipes. Then the pesticides, fertilizers and plant material from the world at large would not stay with him. Makes perfect sense. Still, my eyes begin to glaze over as I listen, knowing that Sam will not be the one doing this. I picture my work schedule shrinking again, every time Chips walks in from outside. At first this idea seems a real pain in the butt, but I can't deny the logic. To discover the cause of the problems, however, allergy testing remains the only alternative. "Shaving the dog's hair and doing scratch tests are one method, but I can assure you it can be done with blood tests alone." Sam and I discuss and agree to the blood tests, on the next visit. Dr. Werner also recommends avoiding wheat, a common allergen, whenever possible.

The Doctor soon finds out what we know very well – Chips isn't the world's most cooperative patient. He won't let anyone probe or poke him without putting up some fight, specifically snapping, his only defense. He doesn't actually make physical contact, but scares anyone holding him enough to call for a muzzle. I hate putting the thing on him, but understand that no vet would sacrifice an arm for my dog's well being, clearly a personality deficit on his part. When we leave the office, a woman waiting for her cat in the reception area asks us "Is he a Tibetan Terrier?"

"We think so."

"I hope you're ready to care for him a long time. My Tibetan lived twenty years." Wow! Sam and I are thrilled to hear that at least some of these dogs lived that long. We want this boy with us as many years as possible. He's such good company to have around. But we know that one person's good luck doesn't bring any guarantees to another.

The allergy test results come back. They're both unsettling and comforting. "You're dog is allergic to almost every single plant that we tested for," Dr. Werner tells us, "including grass, and fleas as well." I also notice on the results that he's allergic to penicillin. Me too! Having noted that he's left-pawed as I am left handed, I begin to wonder if my maternal feelings toward him are pre-determined by something in our DNA. "So if Chips gets even a single flea bite, he'll be scratching and biting for quite a while."

"What can we do?"

"Well, we could make up a vaccine that in sixty percent of the cases helps a lot." We are ready to go for this solution until we learn that the shots we assumed were once a month, had to be given every day at the start, then every other day and so on. "Most owners give them themselves" he tells us.

"But we can barely put in ear drops together. He's so uncooperative." Probably, in his practice, Dr. Werner was used to dealing with more dogs who've had good homes from puppyhood. He could see that Chips' personality, which had been through at least some trauma, would not easily accommodate to daily or even weekly shots.

"You could bring him into the office for them." I knew that would be very time consuming in Los Angeles traffic. We live on the West side, and Dr. Werner is in the Valley. "But with his personality, you might want to try the paw cleaning and medications for a while, and see how that goes." We opt for the latter as the best idea for the moment.

The royal paw washing goes into effect immediately. With his large, well padded feet, toes and pads interspersed with hair, Chips picks up all manner of burrs and plant material, also the occasional worm. In the mornings, when everyone in the neighborhood turns on sprinklers, he comes back with wet as well as dirty paws. A quick wipe not being enough, I get two large bowls, fill them with warm water, put them on the floor of the small back room, and proceed to ask Chips to come over to have his feet washed.

Strange as it may seem, Chips does not jump at the chance to have some writer attending to his feet. At first this ritual seems to actually embarrass him. He looks around as if it's some indignity to which he's being subjected. Fortunately, his face seems to say, this humiliation was not being witnessed by canine friends in the neighborhood. "My lowly position on the floor here doesn't concern you in the least, does it?" Sitting next to the bowls, I feel like a handmaiden about to wash some titled being's feet. And it isn't easy getting Chips to come near enough the bowls for me to lift him a little under the legs and place one paw at a time in them.

After a few weeks of the paw washing, however, Chips must realize that this process is non-negotiable.

Two paws get washed in each bowl. After one foot is done, and the not infrequent burr, worm or tree berry removed, I dry it with a towel, going between each toe as best I can. It seems like a long routine, but I become so efficient, that the whole business usually lasts no more than three minutes. Thank God afternoon walks are a drier and less messy affair; afterward, Chips' feet require only a quick wipe with a wet towel or Babywipe.

Although not thrilled about this whole experience at first, Chips soon comes to accept and then maybe enjoy it, realizing, I hope, that the foot bath feels better than all the chewing and licking he'd previously done. After a month, when I say "let's do the footsies," Chips trudges after me into the back room. A few months later, he actually lies down, turns on his side and sticks out his four paws. It's comical, but he needs to be righted into a standing position to get the bowls involved.

The whole procedure immediately improves his feet along with our relationship. In short, he apparently finds something positive in this strange ritual we have in the mornings – every time I finish, he begins rubbing his sides around me, leaning against my back, going under my arms and being generally playful, waiting for a couple of hugs and kisses, which I always include as a kicker. The bond between us strengthens with all these small routines. Probably a few kings of yore and their servants knew such ties.

Amazingly, no matter how far out his bath gets, Chips always smells great. I don't know whether it's his breed, the food he gets or his own individual perfume, but he has to be the best smelling dog on earth. Sometimes I put my face in his hair or kiss his head, inhaling the always sweet aroma. Those few other individuals who get close to him also comment on this attribute. Even his breath smells sweet. A kiss from him would have been welcome. Although a non-licker, Chips shows affection in all sorts of other ways. In retrospect, I realize that I could easily have trained him to lick us by putting a bit of peanut butter on my face or hand. But if it doesn't come naturally to him, why do it? We could live with Chips' own brand of affection quite happily.

The allergies, despite all our efforts, remain a continuous struggle. Being an allergist, human or animal, is a winning medical career in L.A. More people and dogs have them here than I've ever noticed on the East Coast. With Chips we don't let the problem get out of hand. Using the medication the dermatologist suggests for a few days, then weaning him off it gradually seems to work best. But when on even the small amount of steroids, Chips' appetite increases tremendously. Our communications about food become refined during these periods, with him licking his mouth to indicate hunger. I'd experienced the same hunger when I once took steroids. When taking the medicine Chips gets more food and more frequent feedings, which soon reinforce his understanding of how to get me to the refrigerator. In two seconds, he knows the phrase "Are you're hungry?" Anytime I ask him if he's hungry, he runs to the refrigerator or licks his mouth.

Naturally, his allergies require bathing in special anti-itch soaps and conditioners. His new shampoo costs twenty-five dollars bottle, his conditioner even more, but that's o.k. because my own shampoo, from Trader Joe's, is much, much cheaper. If I lump our total hair cleaning expense together, it isn't too bad. Dr. Werner also tells us that one of the two popular flea preventatives comes in a spray as well as the concentrated dose for between the shoulders. "The spray works better for a dog with sensitive skin. No matter how distasteful using a pesticide sounds, flea prevention, especially for an allergic dog, is the most important line of defense."

Chips tolerates the new spray much better than the spot liquid. Sam, though detesting using these chemicals on our clean pet, takes it upon himself to actually do the nasty, monthly deed, while I hold Chips on the leash with a washcloth over his face to protect it. Whenever the spray and gloves come out, Chips heads for his best hiding place – the hole. One wonders how dogs and cats rationalize these unpleasant things we do to them. Here we are, creatures that normally improve their lives, suddenly taking a turn for the worse. Inevitably, Sam uses the spray too sparingly I believe. And every single time he does this, he mutters something about "...poisoning the dog." But the stuff seems to keep fleas away.

One day I look in Chips' medicine cabinet, a shelf in my kitchen closet, holding his vitamins, fifteen assorted drops, tablets, ointments, and sprays – for ear infections, allergies, medications, both conventional and herbal, skin infection pills, steroid-antihistamine pills, plain antihistamines of various types, tranquilizer pills for long journeys in the car and so forth. Was he an especially sick animal or were we hypochondriacal on his behalf? I've since discovered that many of our responsible pet owning friends have similar shelves for their dogs and cats. Like all of us, pets have health issues. Luckily, we don't have to pay for college or a wedding.

In the meantime, I finish the script rewrite for A&E, but now the president of the film division leaves, and with his departure go most of his projects in development, including ours. I'm back to looking for a home for John's wonderful story. In the meantime, here is Chips, making each day better than it would otherwise be. What a wonderful consolation dogs are in times of insecurity.

Chapter 16

DOGGY WANT ADS

---

*I had rather see the portrait of a dog that I know,
than all the allegorical paintings
they can show me in the world.*

SAMUEL JOHNSON

Every bright creature needs something to do. And like all dogs, Chips obviously craves activity, maybe a job. More than most dogs, he lies around looking depressed much of the time that I'm working. This changes when I take him somewhere or sit outside with him. His dozen toys are of no interest and, except after our tennis games, playing with a ball not on his radar screen. After all, he doesn't see any humans chasing balls because he's never been to a baseball game, clearly a deficit for which we're responsible.

Though toys generally do not tempt him, when I'm shopping he seems to find decorative teddy bears on low shelves irresistible. "I think your dog wants that bear" one young woman tells me in a clothing store. I turn around to find Chips dragging a teddy bear off a shelf and proceeding to chew on it. "Sorry." Obviously, I have to buy the thing now that he's gotten his saliva on it. "How much is it" I ask.

"Oh, it's not for sale, but I suppose that I could sell it. How's twenty-five dollars?" I figure that I got away cheap all things considered. This bear is almost as big as Chips. Another time, in another store, he manages to pull another decorative teddy bear off a shelf. The most attention these Teddies get at home is enough to have their ears, and perhaps a nose chewed off. Afterwards, they remain untouched for the rest of their noseless, earless lives.

Chips always wants to do whatever we do. Whenever I'm stretching in our back room, he gets down on the floor with me, rolling on his back to simulate my moves. Generally he just lies around. I know that's what dogs mostly do, but Chips' keen interest in everything human seems to beg for a higher level of satisfaction.

I look in the paper. There are no want ads for dogs, so it's a challenge to find him meaningful work. I already tried and failed to train him to bring in the newspaper. Coming up with nothing for our boy to enjoy outside of his walks frustrates me. When I sit at the computer writing for more than an hour or two, Chips looks totally bored, occasionally sighs, although he never strays from my office, no matter how long I work there. Only when he hears my text saving function whirr does he get up and stretch, knowing I'll finally be leaving the computer.

Dogs' intelligence and energy have little outlet. Inevitably they are left alone a lot; even those with canine companions are happiest when actually doing some activity. That's why the walks to new places, runs on the beach, in the woods or playing in a dog park rise to such importance. I'd heard about a canine agility class near the airport and thought that might suit Chips. He's a terrific jumper into cars and onto furniture.

Though shortage of time is always a problem, I feel obliged to pursue this pastime for Chips. One afternoon I phone, only to be told that the classes were suspended for the moment, but to bring Chips over to see if he likes the course. At this facility, a friendly young woman shows us to the outdoor area where the agility equipment is set up. It looks like a canine playground. "Why don't you put Chips on or over the small structures?" With her help, I get him on see-saws, over jumps, on various obstacles, and finally through a wavy tunnel sort of thing.

"Good boy" we both say. He goes through the whole course easily, hesitating only at the tunnel, until I call him from the far end.

"Terrific!" the young woman says. "He's a natural." I know that Chips jumps quite high, but never realized he had such good balance and coordination. I grow excited. Here is an activity made for him.

"But I don't have any classes right now," the woman reminds me, interrupting my daydreams of Chips' flying over jumps. "I'm losing my lease here and will have to see about finding another place." Like a bucket of cold water her words wash away that fantasy for the moment. The young woman takes my number and promises to call if she manages to get another set-up. But now that I've found this perfect diversion for Chips, I'm not about to give up easily. Doing things like this with Chips makes me feel like a kid again. Dogs tend to do this – pull us back to childhood or some exhilarating time when we feel none of the inhibitions we acquire later on.

I call around to my canine contacts and discover another agility place about a half hour's drive from our house. As anyone who's lived in L.A. knows, a normal half hour ride with heavy traffic is two, even three times as long, but, hey, Chips needs a job. After my glowing report to Sam on Chips' athletic skills, he wants to see them himself.

We three enter an indoor facility with similar agility equipment to the first place, but it's all inside a fenced indoor area. Dogs are going through their paces on agility structures. When it isn't being used for these classes, the area is apparently cleared and used for doggy day care, with the animals socializing while their guardians work or vacation.

Sam and I anticipate Chips' delight in coming here, my husband trusting the account I'd given. As we enter the facility, our boy is on high alert. I try to lead him through the gate, but Chips plants his feet and pulls back on the leash. Instead of focusing on the agility activities, he seems to see only the big pen. A gated area with dogs inside probably means one thing to him – a pound. Though I manage to finally entice Chips inside, he remains anxious, showing no interest in the course.

While other dogs go up, through or over the various obstacles, Chips only wants to socialize with them.

Despite my repeated efforts to get him on the equipment, he ignores or walks around it, becoming intermittently nervous. I take him out of the fenced area to watch the other dogs, hoping that this will encourage him to participate in the same things they're doing. No success. The activity he took to with no other dogs or distractions near the airport was of zero interest to him when other dogs were around. I come back another day with him, but he wants nothing to do with this place.

The original young woman teacher never finds a facility. I finally discover one other agility possibility about two hours away, but it too closes for good before I even get there. There are no other agility courses in our area or any adjacent ones that I can find. Perhaps we give up too easily. That is the end of agility, but not of my search for a canine job.

Several people mention to me that Chips would make a wonderful therapy dog for folks in the hospital. Many hospitals and nursing homes have programs for visiting pets. It's great for the patients and for the dogs who seem to sense what good they're doing; they actually thrive on the attention. Maybe Chips would feel he's earned his kibble. I hear about an informational meeting concerning the certification process.

I drive to Santa Monica to learn about the Delta Society, which certifies therapy dogs. Certification requires that both "owners" and pets pass tests. The guardians must study a book and video while the pets are examined by Delta Society appointees. Again, I question whether I have the time for all this, but know that Chips would enjoy actually doing some new activity with me. So I order the book and video, study the course, take the written tests and prepare Chips for his big evaluation. His "studies" involve witnessing people making noise or seeing them create a disturbance, as might happen in a hospital, and not reacting.

A friend helps me out, practicing with Chips by knocking over a metal chair to simulate the sound of a wheelchair or walker, and yelling as a frustrated patient might. Chips seems to be o.k. with both. We repeat these incidents several times, with Chips continuing to only show mild interest; he remains calm. I'm excited at the prospect of my boy and me sharing something new together.

After making the appointment for our test, preparing my appearance and greeting style as suggested, I groom Chips and get him ready for the big moment. The day before our test date, I run into another pet "owner" whose dog is already certified. She tells me that if you're visiting a facility in another city with a certified therapy dog, he's allowed on the plane. In the body of the plane! What an added bonus this would be for us. We travel and would love to take Chips with us, especially to visit New York, where I have family. The usual twelve pound limit for dogs on a plane leaves us out...unless we cut Chips in half and take him in two carry-ons. Needless to say, we would never cage him and put him in the luggage compartment. We'd heard too many horror stories about what sometimes happens, though usually it doesn't.

Sam wishes us good luck as we drive off for our exam. There's a lot riding on this. I'm nervous as we reach the small house in Santa Monica where our examination is scheduled. I hope that Chips doesn't catch my anxiety. We enter to find several dogs waiting there in cages. I have no idea why. Did they belong to the people running this operation? Were they awaiting their turns for exams? Chips immediately notices them, makes his crying noise and becomes agitated, alert. Not a good beginning. I try to calm him. While several examiners watch us, one woman approaches me with outstretched hand. I meet her gaze, shake her hand and smile warmly as instructed in the Delta course book.

I introduce myself and Chips before she tells me they're beginning the exam. She goes back across the room and starts walking toward us in a crazy way, arms and legs moving way up and down like a robot, leaning from side to side as she makes some strange noise. When the woman gets close to us, Chips walks behind me and stays there. The other examiners watching turn thumbs down. That's right. They actually hold up their hands and turn their thumbs down, as in the Roman Forum. I feel like a prisoner who's just been condemned to become dinner for the lions. I bring Chips back around front. "We'll try again," she says. Once more, this woman repeats the whole act, approaching us with the same bizarre walk. I honestly have never seen anyone in a hospital move this way, but these people have their testing methods down pat. Once again Chips hides behind me. Up go the hands and down go the thumbs.

"We're sorry, but he's too fearful," another woman tells me. That was it. In two seconds, Chips and I are on the sidewalk, having been rejected, failing to live up to the grade. My dreams of Dr. Chips ministering to patients with his sweet presence are dashed. As we head back to the car, I call Sam to give him the bad news.

"We flunked."

"I don't believe it." Naturally, he's shocked that anyone wouldn't want his wife and dog team on their side.

As we head home I assure Chips that he's a "very good boy."

After the agility and therapy fiascos, I'm still determined to find our dog something to do. Therapy seems just the ticket, regardless of our first rejection. Close to where we live are two world class hospitals with their own dog therapy programs. They do not require certification from the Delta Society. I go to one of the hospitals and talk to the volunteer office. "We have a lot of dogs in the program, but none like this one," the woman in charge tells me while petting Chips. She finds him irresistible. "Would you be willing to go to the Aids floor?"

"We'll go wherever you want," I assure her. I fill out numerous forms.

"We'll call when there's an opening on the schedule." After a few months we do get a call and are instructed to come in for an examination by the vet. It's a behavioral exam to determine whether the dog is o.k. being touched by strangers. When we reach the hospital, we're directed to an outdoor area where the head of the volunteer program and the vet will meet us. I hold my breath.

The male vet pets and touches Chips in several ways. All's well. Yes, I think, we're going to make it. "He seems fine," the woman tells me. "Part of the exam includes the vet taking the leash from the guardian and walking the dog away. What? We're at the Rubicon. I know that Chips will never let anyone walk him in a direction away from me.

"Why is this necessary," I ask as Chips' leash is taken by the vet.

"In case someone needs to take him from you," the head of volunteers tells me. Chips starts to whimper and turns his head back toward me.

"But why would that happen?" My heart sinks seeing Chips pulling away from the vet.

"In case you have to go to the bathroom, for instance."

"Oh, he can come with me," I assure her. "After all I watch him going to the toilet." But that doesn't fly. Unless Chips will walk away with the vet, he could not pass their test. And Chips definitely refuses to do this. He would stay with someone to whom I handed the leash, but not walk away from where he left me. It seems silly to ask the dog to do something that will never really come up while visiting the hospital. But once again, we are determined to not be up to snuff. Poor Chips. Unemployed and bored again. But there is one more hospital program to try. UCLA has its own program.

While mulling over our next attempt at the therapy dog gig, Chips continues visits to Poa, his friend around the corner. The dogs still have a good time together. Poa, a few years older than Chips has acquired diabetes. She needs daily shots, which our friends give her. A year or two after she starts the shots her eyesight pretty much goes. Poa continues enjoying life, though, especially visits to Santa Barbara where our friends have a weekend house.

Unfortunately, during Poa's last trip there she is brutally attacked for no reason by another dog. The aggressive dog apparently jumped out of a car belonging to someone visiting our friends. Poa, unable to see, was just sunbathing in the yard when the attack took place. Despite emergency surgery and a subsequent visit to her vet in L.A., Poa pretty much gives up at that point, she never recuperates. Our friends are sadly forced to put her to sleep.

After mourning the loss of their wonderful pet they begin thinking about another dog. I suggest Perfect Pet Rescue, where we'd found Chips. One visit to see the dogs is all it takes for them to adopt Koko, an adorable, small female mix who looks like a cross between a Poodle and Terrier. Chips meets Koko, who clearly likes him, even licking his face and following him around. But, he plays his hard to get routine, running around their yard with Koko trailing after him.

One weekend when our friends are out of town, I volunteer to walk Koko, who's staying at her own house with a housekeeper. I know Koko will enjoy going out with Chips and vice versa. Chips, as usual, pulls me toward her front door as soon as we round the corner near her house. She greets him with a lick on his face and seems delighted to trot along with us. But you would never know from his walking demeanor that Chips was anxious to see her too. Men! He basically ignores her, but seems content to have her follow along with him. Typical macho behavior. We continue our visits with the gentle Koko despite Chips' cool attitude. I try to make up the affection to Koko that Chips doesn't dish out. We girls have to stick together.

Chapter 17

A MATTER OF WILL

In relations between humans and animals, it is always the human that is in debt.

ROGER GRENIER

Five years of doggy delights pass. We drive with Chips to Carmel to see our friend, Sidney, who happens to be our attorney as well. He specializes in wills and estates – and both of ours need rewriting. We have not updated them since we've been married. For one thing, we want to provide for Chips in case the two of us go at once, as in a plane crash. The amount of money put aside has to be generous without sounding crazy. A few years after this, Leona Helmsley's will, in which she left something like twelve million dollars for her dog, was overturned. The court in fact gave some of the money to her grandchildren, whom she had specifically and purposely disinherited. That seems very wrong.

Then there was the case of the cat whose fifty thousand dollar bequest was overseen by an executor. The "owner," having thought it all through, assigned an executor to dole out the money periodically to the housekeeper who was caring for the cat after the "owners" demise. When the cat died, the house-keeper merely went out and obtained another one who looked very much like the first, so that the money would continue to flow her way. She never informed the executor that the first cat died. Eventually, her ruse was discovered.

I'm not worried about someone cheating Chips of proper care in order to pocket extra cash. Our friends and families are more honest and honorable than that. They include many, if not all, animal lov-ers. The problem we have is picking the right per-son or persons for the caretaking. Almost everyone we know likes Chips and many are willing to sign on as guardians-to-be. But the question on our minds is who would care for him as we do.

"How about Berta" Sam asks.

"First of all, her building doesn't allow pets and she really is not strong enough to walk him."

"You're right. How about my other sister?"

"She and her husband are definitely animal lovers but never walk their dog." To be fair, their Maltese actually hates to walk on a leash, is small enough to get a lot of exercise in their yard, and doesn't like other dogs. "And Ginger doesn't like Chips or other dogs much."

"True. How about your brother?" Sam asks me.

"I don't know if he wants a dog. And Chips isn't used to the cold weather in New York."

Next, we go through our list of friends in California, just about all dog lovers. To my first suggestion, Sam says, "she gives her dog nothing but kibble, and would never do the cooking that Chips is used to."

Sam has another idea. "Steve and Arlene?"

"But their dog gets out all the time and once got hit by a car."

"Right. I forgot that. How about..." and he names other friends.

"They restrict their dog to two rooms, which drives him crazy."

"That's not for our guy." I suggest another couple.

"Don't you remember that they left their dog in a kennel when they went to Europe. He stopped eating, lost fifteen pounds and got fleas."

"I didn't know that!" And so it went, on and on. No one, we realize, would actually do things exactly as we wanted.

"Maybe he should be euthanized when we die. Then it won't be a problem and he won't suffer without us."

"No vet will put a perfectly healthy dog to sleep."

"One with no scruples would."

"So you want Chips to be put down by some money grubbing, unprincipled vet whom he doesn't know!?" This conversation was getting us nowhere. It reminded me of an "Everyone Loves Raymond" episode, in which Ray and his wife are discussing whom to leave their children to if they both died at once. After each eliminated the other's family, they began going through their friends, all of whom had significant enough flaws which put them out of the running. Then the wife said to Ray, something like, "who do we know who's responsible, sensitive, fun, intelligent, talented and kind?"

"If we know anyone like that we should give them the kids right now," Ray answers.

Sam and I do not come to an agreement that day, but at least settle on an amount of money that would have taken good care of Chips for as long as he might live. When we return home, I write a little booklet for the mythical, perfect, future guardian, with extensive instructions and suggestions on "the care and feeding of Chips."

Our challenge remains one facing many dog guardians. Questions such as whom to leave one's dog to or who gets him in a divorce are today anticipated by many couples getting married. I understand that more and more prenuptial agreements contain stipulations about the allocation of rights by the two parties regarding their four legged charges in case of divorce.

In New York City, lawyer Eleanor Alter told the New York Times "I did one prenup [Eleanor Alter recalled it as a separation agreement] with nine pages just on the joint-custody issue of their Dandie Dinmont Terrier. One party had primary custody, but the other had visitation rights. If the dog was bred, the one without custody had first pick of the litter."

In the book, "Dearest Pet: On Bestiality" by Midas Dekkers, (Verso, 2000) another divorce case mentioned one joint custody agreement in which a fellow "...Ben Miller now picks up Bruce, age five, every

Friday evening from his ex-wife in the suburbs of New York and returns the Collie on Sunday."

Another divorce case resulted in a judgment in which the wife was given custody of the dog "with reasonable visiting rights for the spouse. 'We are both determined that he suffer no adverse affects from being the product of a broken home. We don't tell ugly tales about each other, or attempt to bribe his affections with showers of tasty treats, fancy dog apparel or extended bouts of fetch-the-stick.' "

Thank God we didn't have to deal with Chips' custody in a divorce. That might have necessitated months of legal wrangling. As to our will, we eventually decide that Sam's younger sister and her husband were probably the best bet. Sam knows that they'd honor his wishes to walk Chips or arrange to have him walked at least twice per day. The rest of their caretaking would be wonderful because they genuinely love dogs and are always affectionate toward Chips. Additionally, they'd have our voluminous instructions written "for the lucky couple that would get him." Also, his sister and brother-in-law's Maltese is older than Chips and may not last as long.

We hope, of course, to outlive our dog so that he will never have to adjust to life without us. Maybe, if anyone bothered to ask him, Chips might say that life wasn't that great in Beverly Hills – no beaches, too many restrictions at restaurants, no Diggidy Dog! But for now, he has no other option.

Chapter 18

NO BOW WOW IN BUDAPEST

*In relations between humans and animals, it is
always the human that is in debt.*

ROGER GRENIER

During our next visit to Carmel I notice that my
boy chews on his butt here and there. Now that's just
not something a refined guy like Chips ever does. It's
clearly not a normal leisure pastime such as licking
one's privates, but some irritation that makes him kind
of jump and chew. Being the mommy, I of course have
to examine the situation. No doubt there is irritation,
maybe an infection. I call the vet in L.A. who tells
me to try some pills which I dutifully get from a local
vet; he concurs with the treatment. The problem goes

away, but a week later returns. We follow this routine at least three times with the result being the same. A higher level of action clearly is indicated.

We try to make an appointment at the University of California at Davis, the top notch veterinary college about four hours away. They don't have any time available soon, so I call a friend of mine who just happens to be a large donor to the school. After all, if people can get their children into colleges with connections and contributions, why shouldn't we try all of our possibilities for the suffering Chips? Strings must be pulled where possible. "A donation from you would help also," our friend lets me know.

"Sure. We'll do that." It's getting complicated and expensive already. This lady kindly makes a contact to get a good doctor to attend to Chips. The only time they can make for him is in the morning a few days later. The trip requires an overnight stay at a questionable motel – its only recommendation being that they accept dogs. Chips doesn't even want to jump on the bed there, preferring the cleanliness and safety of his own, which we've brought along. I consider this admirable discrimination on his part.

The next morning we arrive at U.C. Davis, fill out the required forms and are ushered into an examination room. The doctor comes in with four veterinary students. Sam and I are on edge even more than usual because we're worried that all these people will scare Chips. The doctor listens to our problem, asks us to put him on the examination table and looks at the area in question himself. "Now, we have to go in and examine him" he tells us. "We will not be hurting him, I assure you. It will just be a little uncomfortable." Would Chips come to the same conclusion? I guess the vet took one look at us and knew we'd be suffering right along with our boy.

The doctor takes care of business quickly and announces, "He's got very deep anal glands. They need to be expressed." A strange turn of phrase, if you ask me. I've heard it before but still find it odd. I know of "anal personalities" and "anal retentive," but "expressing anal glands" still strikes the ear oddly, one of the many new areas of knowledge you learn from having a dog.

"I always thought the groomer took care of that."

"Well, in some dogs the glands are too deep for them to really manage it properly, and Chips is one of those. It's best to have only the vet do it in these cases." I nod obediently. Naturally, Chips would have something inconvenient to handle. This veterinarian explains everything to his students while, in a brief additional maneuver, removing the offending material from Chips' ever so deep glands. The whole business takes five minutes after which I lift Chips off the table.

"Then the irritation is just from chewing ," Sam asks.

"That's right. He should stop that now that he's more comfortable."

After paying a surprisingly small bill, handing over the promised contribution and getting some medication to resolve the current infection, we all leave and drive back to Carmel. That is the last time we ever had to address that particular problem. But we knew there'd be others.

Since our Davis visit, we now realize that it's time to take Chips in for his "anal expression" every time he begins scooting across the rug, something many pet parents are familiar with. As soon as a dog's glands begin filling up (God knows why) and creating discomfort, he starts to kind of drag his bottom along the floor, a very clear signal about what has to be done.

Gee, if I didn't have a dog I wouldn't know all these utterly fascinating things. What would I ever do with all the extra time not going to vets, groomers, veterinary colleges, leash-free beaches, pet stores and the like? Happily, I wouldn't find out for quite some time.

A few days later, Chips awakens me one night by crying next to my bed. He has never done this. Quietly, without even looking over at Sam, I get out from beneath the covers in an effort not to awaken him. I follow Chips, who is now headed for the kitchen. Once there, he goes to the door for what I assume is a need to get out and pee, but I'm wrong. There, outside the door, is my husband, who occasionally sleepwalks. I rush to open it and find Sam, stark naked, on a cold night, in the backyard. Apparently, he'd wandered out in his usual nighttime state of undress. The door had apparently shut on its own, leaving him locked out. "What a great boy Chips," Sam says, now fully awake and petting our precious lad. Chips is covered with praise and petting while I dig out a cookie for reward.

"I was about to start yelling and banging on the door. But I'm glad I didn't have to because one of our neighbors might have heard me before you did."

"I cannot believe you went outside."

"Me neither, but the cold air is a real waker upper." I looked at the thermometer we have hanging outside the kitchen. It reads fifty degrees.

A few years later, in Budapest on vacation, Sam is not as lucky. I'm sleeping, as is my nasty habit at 3 a.m., in our hotel room when the doorbell to the room rings. Startled, I jump out of bed and answer it. It's Sam! "What are you doing out there?" On one of the rare nights that he's actually in pajamas he had sleep walked into the hallway. The lights on in the halls gradually woke him up as he wandered the long corridors looking for our room. All the corridors at this hotel look exactly alike, so I'm amazed that he was able to find our room in a state of semi-consciousness. "I don't know how I ever found this."

" If Chips were here he might have stopped you."

"Right, but I'm surprised there isn't someone monitoring the cameras. They might have seen me and taken me back sooner. I've been walking around a few minutes." I hadn't noticed before, but there were small cameras mounted in the hallways of the hotel. I guess whoever's monitoring them isn't as reliable as one devoted dog. It seems that wherever we go we end up missing Chips.

Chapter 19

HAUTE CUISINE

---

*The whole aim and purpose of owning a dog is to
love it and be loved by it.*

COLETTE AUDRY

Even though we have no evidence that Chips' allergies are in any way related to food, we could not rule
such things out. After I learned that corn and wheat
are the most common allergens, we gave up buying
him cookies containing those ingredients. And just to
make him feel better, I gave up cookies as well. In our
never ending search for ever better food and allergy
solutions, I hear several times about raw food being
the best for dogs. I remain very skeptical but look into
it. One man with a beautiful dog tells us that "this

guy's luxurious coat and healthy skin are due to the raw diet I give him." Formerly an allergy sufferer, his dog is now free of the problem. We take the name of the woman from whom he purchases the special food.

Our visit to Pat McKay takes a while. We drive almost an hour to get there, enter a kind of warehouse, and find the lady in question. After we explain that Chips has lots of plant allergies, she extols the virtues of raw food with its freshness and superior nutrients. We're talking raw meat and chicken here. We ask about salmonella, e-coli and all those other wonderful things. She poo-poos our concerns, explaining "dogs in the wild ate raw meat all the time."

Well, from what I know, dogs in the wild didn't live too long, certainly not the twelve plus years many of our domestic pets do. Also, animals in the wild, who must kill their prey, eat them immediately, before any bacteria have a chance to invade. But, in about three seconds, Pat whips out a few raw chicken hearts and puts them in a dish. "You'll see how he loves it" she assures us, placing the bowl in front of our dog. Chips sees a bowl on the floor, knows he's being made an offer, walks over to it, sniffs, looks up, sniffs again, glances at us suspiciously and walks away.

"This is some kind of trick, right" he seems to ask. Pat appears surprised. She picks up a couple of raw chicken hearts in her hand and extends it to Chips. "Here boy." Eventually, probably out of politeness (Chips is nothing if not polite} he walks over, sniffs a second longer, but comes right back to us.

"I guess it's not his cup of tea," I say.

"He'll get used to it" she insists. "And his allergy problems will disappear." We're both still skeptical, but agree to try the diet. Our friends Sidney and Lynn have been using the same diet for their small poodles who seem quite healthy. We buy some frozen meat from Pat and a bunch of nutrients. Neither Sam nor I could countenance raw chicken under any circumstances. It just seems too risky. Our own vets don't recommend raw food.

At home, we offer Chips the new uncooked fare several more times, with basically identical results. He tentatively tries it a couple of times, but makes his disdain clear. I begin slightly cooking the stuff, which he likes better. But only after cooking the meat to a normal rare condition do I see him eat with any enthusiasm. I reason that if we we're going to still cook for him, I needn't drive an hour each way to pick up special food. I could simply use our own meat and chicken, which I mix with his kibble. Why shouldn't Chips have something he likes?

While visiting some Miniature Dachshund owning friends, we make a startling discovery – each breed has its own best recipe for food. Their daughter, Diana, a marvelous cook, warms up some concoction for her dogs' dinner. I watch as Chips, who's just finished his own meal, wants to gobble down the smaller dogs' food. He's frantic to get to their bowls. "You'd think he hadn't eaten in a week," I say.

Despite our willingness to make Chips happy in almost any way possible, I retain a modicum of manners – - and restrain him from attacking the other dogs' dishes. "Can I give him some of this" Diana asks. Naturally, we agree. She serves Chips some of the warmed up mixture which he wolfs (dogs?) down in three seconds, then looks at us as if to say "I never knew about this stuff!" Of course absolutely nothing makes our hearts sing like seeing Chips really happy. I want this recipe ASAP.

"I got the recipe from this dog guru who claims to have the best formula for each breed," Diana tells us. "No one breed requires exactly the same recipe as another. Naturally, what's best for a Dachshund is not necessarily good for a Tibetan." She gives me the website and phone number for the man in question. Needless to say, I contact him to get the Tibetan Terrier recipe.

The guy informs me of his hundred dollar fee for each recipe. What?! I could not believe it. I dial Diana, knowing she wouldn't pay such a ridiculous price for a recipe. Wrong again. This otherwise very sensible young woman, who is not a spendthrift, did apparently pony up the exorbitant fee for the secrets of Dachshund nirvana. I thought the whole idea absurd. The man was apparently more into helping his bank account than helping dogs. I refuse to go along with this craziness. We would spend whatever it takes for the best medical care, buy Chips excellent food, get him comfortable beds, plane tickets, harnesses, the lightest collar we could find, but $100.00 for a recipe was beyond the pale, even for me.

Inevitably, predictably, some guilt begins eating away at my conscience while I watch Chips monotonously chewing his kibble, mixed with cooked food. What kind of a mother was I if I wouldn't even try the "ideal recipe" for Tibetans on him? If I could afford it, shouldn't I explore every possibility of improving his life and health, even if I overpay? And Chips, enthusiastic at the beginning, always gets bored with any new kibble I buy. "The best one made," the pet store lady tells me whenever I ask about some new entry in the field. This seems to change every six months or so, when some company comes out with yet another superior "human grade ingredients" food. Sooner or later Chips' enthusiasm always wanes, even though we mix other things into the food. I wonder who wouldn't be bored eating the same thing all the time. But I still give Chips some kibble for his teeth, which I figure might fall out if he doesn't eat anything hard. I could, however, mix the ideal recipe food with the kibble, couldn't I?

Sam and I discuss this "ideal" recipe business and wonder out loud if it might improve Chips' allergies, which always get worse during the spring. Rationalizing that we could afford it and owe our boy the best we can do, I am ashamed to admit that I resentfully order the magic formula. It contains thirteen ingredients including a significant amount of sweet potato! Well, I cook up a whole mess of it -- the shopping, cooking and cleaning, no walk in the park, taking up the better part of a day. I would not do this for Sam or myself. But all through the work I keep thinking how thrilled Chips will be with this stuff. If he loves the Dachshund formula, he should go bonkers over his own perfect food, full of vegetables and meats. I can only imagine.

My anticipation reaches the boiling point by the time I put the gourmet recipe down. Chips walks over, sniffs and begins eating. He doesn't gobble it as wildly as he had the Dachshund formula. And after all my work.... Should I just give him the Dachshund formula? Would his legs grow shorter? For the next few days, Chips' enthusiasm for the new Tibetan recipe begins to wane. I skip the mixture one day in favor of a few small pieces of sliced turkey mixed into his kibble. Gobble, gobble, gobble – it disappears instantly.

I go back to the "platinum" meals, watching my dog's desire for gourmet Tibetan cuisine dissipate with each package. By the time the little packages in my freezer are all gone, so is Chips' excitement. He tolerates the new food, but nothing more. No way would I spend all day cooking up food he barely likes. If I want that kind of rejection, there's always Hollywood. I feel idiotic and embarrassed at conning myself into this whole escapade.

One important thing I did learn from this dog food guru – vitamin C is really bad for dogs. It causes life shortening kidney and liver problems which many dogs have these days. But the pet food companies keep using it because it's a preservative which allows for a longer shelf life. In 1985 the National Research Council concluded after tests that dog food should not include any vitamin C, but in 1994, the pet food governing body, AAFCO, met and decided that they would use it anyway. That was certainly a good piece of information which I now take into account before buying any pet food.

Back to square one: kibble with meat or chicken and veggies. For dessert, Chips has started sharing an apple with Sam at night. They sit in the kitchen together, Sam peeling the skin off Chips' half and cutting it into small pieces. While Sam feeds them to him, eating his own half in between Chips' bites, the two look quite content together. Sometimes I hear my husband talking to him. At these moments I leave the room so they can be together by themselves – - the guys and their nightly apple.

If I'm out walking Chips in the afternoon, and buying myself a frozen yoghurt, my boy gets a tiny tasting cup of that cold treat too. He loves it. One day I spot in the pet store refrigerator, Yoghund, frozen yogurt for dogs. Yes, some enterprising business person has actually had the bright idea of selling frozen yoghurt for dogs. It's made without sugar, with peanut butter with peanut butter and banana in a few flavor variations. It costs almost as much as our nonfat stuff and, of course, Chips loves it. Perhaps the next trend will be pizza for dogs. I know that Chips always wants the pizza we're eating. He gets a little crust, which I realize is a no-no because of the wheat, but refusing his ardent requests simply lies beyond my powers at this point.

Avoiding wheat in dog cookies soon leads us to dry turkey treats. These new healthy snacks drive our pooch wild. But most of them are manufactured in China. Naturally, any country that eats dogs and makes them into hats is unlikely to put its best ingredients into treats for them. This realization set in years before the Chinese pet food scandal. We search for a brand made in the U.S. and ultimately find one, but it has to be mail ordered a dozen packages at a time. Sam takes the ordering upon himself.

And to complete the training of his parents, Chips adds a breakfast coffee ritual. He puts his paws up on Sam's lap one day, while he's drinking his morning coffee, actually cappuccino, after we buy a machine. So Sam offers Chips a taste, which he really likes. From this moment forward, Sam places the last swallow in his cup on the floor, and Chips finishes it off. You'd think that all of this fatherly indulgence would pay off in the dog's preference for him, but Sam still tells me over and over "he's your dog."

For a milisecond I consider getting a female dog who would probably favor Sam, then decide that Chips is enough of a handful for both of us. Sam will simply have to be content with second fiddle status where Chips is concerned.

Chapter 20

PARADISE FOUND AND LOST

Attachments to companion animals defy ordinary logic but conform perfectly to emotional logic.

MICHAEL SCHAFFER

In addition to sitting when he picks up anything in his paw, on his leg or butt, Chips, at about seven, begins to slow down and sit after walking a while. One day he actually arches his back, lowers his head and walks with difficulty. I assume that either his back aches or he's trying to get out of the army. Naturally, we take him to see Dr. Olds, who examines him. "It's his back. Try confining him for a few days and see if he gets better."

Although we still don't like cages for dogs, we put up a baby gate in front of the stairs so that our little guy can't follow us up and down forty times a day. As the gate really sits there unconnected to anything, it could easily be knocked down. Fortunately, Chips doesn't realize this. We also close the door of whatever room we're in to restrict his walking around. A pretty sedentary character anyway, he always lies where I or we are, so that keeping him quiet requires little effort.

Sam carries Chips upstairs at night. A few days later, the dog's back recuperates, but Sam's begins to hurt. He stops carrying the dog up. Though intermittently uncomfortable, Chips' back seems to be working o.k. There's nothing we can do about it anyway. And though neither of us minds giving a tug to our pooch's harness when we think he's being stubborn about directions, we naturally won't pull a dog having back pain. How can we know? Since we don't, Chips, when he sits down, inevitably gets carried back to the car by either Sam or me. Our backs eventually pay the price for this.

Dr. Olds tells us "it would be better to keep Chips off the hills." Well, we live in the hills of Beverly so that a walk now requires driving down a few blocks until we reach a flatter area. It's safer to walk there anyway. Teenagers driving cars in our neighborhood often speed around curves, and no sidewalks exist to protect pedestrians or dogs.

A quick learner, Chips soon understands that if he sits during a walk, he usually gets picked up and carried back to the car. He now has three reasons to sit -- either he's gotten some vegetation or pebble in a paw, his back hurts, or he doesn't want to go where we do – usually toward the car. Naturally, we need to figure out exactly why he's sitting. Chips' flawless sense of direction makes outsmarting him difficult -- no matter how circuitous our route, he always understands when we're trying to aim in the general direction of the car. I finally outsmart him, which is not easy. After he sits, I try to see if he wants to walk in a different direction. If he quickly gets to his feet at that point, the sitting is unrelated to his back or something he picked up. Then I insist that he walks back with me. But if Chips' back really does hurt him, whoever is walking him gets stuck carrying his twenty-five pounds back to the car. This cannot last. <u>We</u> will not last.

Thank God for cell phones. Sam and I begin phoning each other if Chips can't walk anymore, so that whoever is home can drive down and pick up the now sitting or lying Chips. The walking parent returns via the other car. It's an improvement over carrying him. Suddenly, I realize that with back problems, Chips won't be able to walk the long corridors in a hospital like UCLA. Any further therapy dog plans will have to be scrapped.

In my continuing effort to entertain and stimulate Chips, I one day drive to the beach to take him on the walking path next to the sand. A glimpse of ocean, I presume, will lift his spirits. It does that for both of us. But on the way home from Santa Monica, I drive the always packed 405 freeway. When the car in front of me slows, I do too, but the huge old Pontiac behind me doesn't. I'm rear ended and would have ploughed into the car in front of me if I didn't slam on the brakes. Chips, in a rare visit to the front passenger seat, hits the dashboard with his head, then falls off the seat. What have I done? I'm worried about his possibly having a concussion or injury to his healing neck. And I rue the day I gave up on the seatbelt, even though he always got pinned down by it.

The driver of the Pontiac runs over to apologize. "I'm sorry. I just took my eyes off the road for a second." Great. We exchange information and I drive away still worried about Chips. I should have kept him in the back of the car, where it's safer and he goes himself 99% of the time.

Immediately I take Chips over to Dr. Olds. Whether or not his back problem was exacerbated by this accident I have no way of knowing, but he seems o.k. to me and the vet. After the accident, Chips figures out that the front seat is not for him, unless he's being held in someone's lap. He refuses to ride in the front again unless I hold him, which I do when Sam drives. However, *I* have lower back pain the following day. A few incidents of such pain in my previous life have always been resolved by one or two visits to a chiropractor. This time, my back problem remains.

The following summer, we go up to visit Carmel again, renting a house for a month. The rental options for dog guardians are severely limited, but we find a small first floor for rent in an older house that suits us just fine. Chips sees dogs cavorting on the leash-free beach in this canine paradise, and immediately begins whining to go down. By now his neck has fused. Enough time has passed so that Dr. Olds feels it's safe to let him run on the hard packed sand next to the water, but not on soft sand.

Trepidatiously, I take Chips down the long flight of stairs to the beach, praying he will stay in the immediate area of the ocean. I walk him on leash to the water's edge. As soon as I snap the leash off, he races

215

down along the water as I've never seen him run, still barking at the waves when they break. With occasional glances backward to make sure I'm still in sight, Chips enjoys himself immensely. Having him relish the freedom to run along the ocean thrills me. At last, a really happy dog, Chips interacts with other four legged beachcombers, but wants to keep moving down the sand, right at the ocean's edge. How good it feels to see him actually behaving like a normal dog, not fearful, not weak, not injured. I don't want to push our luck the first time out, so I call him back after ten minutes. He doesn't come until a second call combined with my heading in the other direction. Then he bounds toward me with his open-mouthed "smile," ears flying behind him. All is well.

Sam, always more cautious and worried about the dangers any adventure harbors than I, joins in on the next beach visit. He wants to see the uncharacteristically joyful boy I'd described to him. I take a photo of Chips running toward us on the sand that day, which becomes the front of our holiday card at the end of the year. We get more compliments on that photo than on anything else we've ever sent.

But Chips' pleasure soon ends. After the third beach visit, he begins arching his back again and having trouble walking up the long staircase back to the street. Now I know we're in for it. I telephone Dr. Olds in Los Angeles. "Chips should have an immediate neurological examination to see if any damage shows to the neck." My guilt kicks in big time. After all, I'm the one who initiated the beach adventure.

Through our veterinarian friends in Salinas, we locate a veterinary neurologist in Capitola, about an hour from Carmel. I hold my breath while the Doctor examines Chips and concludes "there doesn't seem to be any damage to his neck." I begin breathing again. "I think it's his back." Sam feels tempted to let the neurologist have a go at <u>his</u> back as long as we're there, but restrains himself. Once more, we have to confine our boy to the house we're renting for a few days until he recuperates, give him some special low dose aspirin and stay at home with him whenever we can.

The new beach visits must be stopped. I'm as disappointed about it as Chips, my mood always affected by his. We began giving him glucosamine and chondroitin for his back. I figure if it works for him, I'll take some too. At any rate, he can no longer enjoy the greatest fun he's ever experienced, but only observe others running and playing from the path above the beach. It breaks my heart to watch him looking at the other dogs cavorting below. When he again walks there, he whines near the stairs, but we do no more about it this summer. We hate denying him this fun, but obviously we have no choice if we want him to be able to walk.

I conclude that, after eliminating the beach possibilities due to his back, Chips obviously needs more indulgence in other areas of his life. About this time, Diggedy Dog, a new pet store, opens in Carmel, selling all sorts of accoutrements for the well heeled dog. Barrels of every variety of dog cookie and treat lie temptingly in bins on the floor. Naturally, the dogs want to sniff and taste them. No better marketing tool exists. Chips quickly learns the route to this store from any point in Carmel. Wherever we are, he tries to lead us there, even figuring out shortcuts through alleys and alternate routes. We feel that with the beach now being a forbidden zone for Chips, we have to maximize his remaining pleasures, so he always gets to go into the store and "buy" something. When the owner sees us coming she knows it's a sure sale. But true to his refined nature, Chips never grabs a treat from the bins. I'm amazed. He has more self control than I would, given the same position. Chips sniffs everything, but if he really wants it, he stays in front of that basket and looks up at me. Need I say that's all it takes?

If we walk Chips after dinner, it's always in town as there are no streetlights in the residential areas. Though a marvelous way to see the stars, the total darkness in residential Carmel at night makes it difficult to maneuver without a flashlight. But with or without the streetlights, Chips unfailingly finds his way to the certain temptations of Diggidy Dog, his new favorite spot. We obviously can't explain that the store is closed. He needs to see for himself. Invariably, Chips walks up to the door and paws it. I rattle the door to show him it's locked. And though he sits and looks through the glass door at the deserted store, the fact that it's still lit up makes him unsure that it's a lost cause. "I'm sorry," I tell him. He understands that phrase as I'd used it many times to indicate something disappointing to him.

Speaking of "conversations" with Chips, whenever I say something he doesn't understand, he turns his head sideways and gives me a quizzical look. People who talk to their dogs a lot know that they understand many phrases. They also find out what it is to get strange looks in the street.

Chapter 21

BACK TO BACK TO BACK

---

*The great evolutionary success of their species lies in
their ability to convince us our need for them.*

MARK DOTY

At the end of the summer, when we return to
L.A., Sam's back is giving him more problems. What
is it with our family? We're shortly scheduled to go
with some friends to the film festival in San Sebas-
tian, Spain. Everything's booked and mostly paid for.
Berta would stay with Chips, the walkers are lined up
and Sam is anxious to see the Basque countryside for
the first time. Though he's not in the best of shape, we
leave for vacation.

Traveling in Spain with Sam is wonderful as he's able to speak to a lot of the locals. His back pain, however, gets progressively worse with each day. Unable to walk too far without sitting, Sam eventually starts dragging his leg. We finish the trip knowing we have to get to a doctor immediately upon our return.

In L.A., visits to a neurologist and orthopedic surgeon indicate that Sam should start a program of intense physical therapy and injections to avoid surgery. Weeks of these go by, but he never improves. Walking becomes a real challenge.

It turns out that the orthopedist, Dr. Goldstein, truly loves dogs. We spot a beautiful, black Standard Poodle in his private office one day, and begin talking about dogs with him. Sam shows him a photo of Chips which he carries in his wallet. "Bring him the next time you come in" the doctor tells us. "Of course, you'll have to use the back door." And we do just that.

Dr. Goldstein and Chips get on very well. Not surprisingly, Chips makes friends with the whole staff there. I always knew he'd do well in a medical setting. The doctor gives Chips a little white stuffed camel with a squeaker in it to take home. Though never big on toys, he always favored that camel above all others. From then on, almost every time we go to Dr. Goldstein's office, Chips gets to come along. In addition to being a terrific doctor and human being, his canine leanings naturally endear him to us all the more.

Sam's other options eventually exhausted, surgery has to finally be scheduled. Once more, we impose on Berta to stay with Chips for a few days so that I can be at the hospital. When Sam comes home I try holding Chips back from jumping on him while he slowly gets out of the car. I pick our boy up to let him see Sam's face. For the first time ever, Chips welcomes him with a quick swipe of his tongue across Sam's nose. "He's never kissed <u>me</u>" I say, trying to point out Chips tremendous love for Sam. We can't believe it. He must really have missed his Dad. Since then, Chips has repeated this small nose lick ONLY when we return from vacations or hospitals. That's the extent of his kissing repertoire.

Post surgery, Sam stays home for a while without going out. Chips appreciates this constant company, and his attention to Sam indicates that he recognizes his vulnerability. We begin calling him "Dr. Chips," though his practice is confined to one patient. I suspect that Sam must talk wine with him when they're alone because, after that, every time Sam goes to his wine closet in the dining room, Chips does too. Although our little guy doesn't know his Beaujolais from a Chardonnay, he's certainly interested in the contents of that closet. Of course the fact that we're now keeping his treats and kibble in there, at the wine's ideal 55 degrees, might have something to do with it. We had decided that merely room temperature might not be ideal for maintaining his food's freshness.

Sam's post-operative physical therapy helps him gradually improve. But any more lifting of Chips onto the bed or into cars, has to be done by moi. Unfortunately for me, our walks occasionally still end with my carrying him back to the car. This doesn't help my back either, the only decent one left in the family. We ask Dr. Olds "Is there any way to find out exactly what's wrong with Chips' back? We want to know what, if anything, can be done about it. "

"The only way to really know is another MRI." We surely don't want to put Chips through that again, another procedure with anesthesia. But how else would we ever find out what's wrong with him? Ignorance is not always bliss. This MRI would be a spinal one, to determine exactly how extensive the problem might be. After mulling it over, we decide that since we can afford it, we owe Chips the advantage of a proper diagnosis. Again, we think of all the dogs whose "owners" do not have that luxury. Those animals would remain undiagnosed, possibly mistreated, or, if circumstances are bad enough, put to sleep.

Back to the MRI center. This time we're granted a discount on the original fee, since we'd been there before. I again regret the day that we passed up the chance to get pet insurance. The radiologist gives Chips a shot to anesthetize him, and we hold him while the medication takes effect. When he's definitely out, the doctor carries his limp body away from us.

Naturally, we're nervous during the several hours the procedure takes. To be unconscious for that long requires a lot of medication, which might, we thought, have a permanent damaging effect. Time crawls by endlessly. We keep checking hour after hour. We don't understand why it takes so long. One of the assistants explains that "the smaller spine of the dog requires the machine to work much more slowly than on humans, with all those little bones and tissues." We remember hearing that before. For Sam and me, the three hours feel like six. We're wrecks.

Finally, Chips begins coming out of the anesthesia. I hold him and put on his collar and harness while his weakened body struggles to get away from me. I am amazed at how strongly he fights to leave my arms while I put on his paraphernalia. I won't let him go no matter how he tries. Finally, I realize why. Chips begins to pee as he comes out of the anesthetic. He looks totally humiliated as he piddles on the floor next to me. This dog has NEVER had an accident in our house. No way he wants to pee near me if he can avoid it, but I didn't give him a choice. "I'm sorry," I tell him as he looks sadly into my eyes. "You're a good boy." One of the clinic's assistants takes care of the floor.

The radiologist hands us the MRI to carry to the surgeon. Dr. Olds studies the images and explains, "Chips has four herniated disks."

"No wonder he can't walk too far."

"Too much to operate. It would be cruel." I break out in a cold sweat, as I'm sure Sam does. The words seemed like the nails in the coffin of Chips' pleasure. Would our dog lose his ability to run or walk? "They are mild and medium herniations," Dr. Olds says. "Let him just do the best he can. But no walking up hills."

That should be simple. It only means that we can't any longer walk to town or back from the street near the beach when we visit Carmel. We're already driving to his walks in L.A. Also, Chips' sitting during walks would definitely have to be taken seriously. Whether he stops because of something in his paw, on his leg, stubbornness about our direction or pain from his back, we need to know. But being close to him makes that easier. We can read him and vice versa.

Chips' stops are now categorizable. A sudden sit down in the middle of a walk indicates he's picked something up which bothers him. Easy enough. Until I take it out or off, Chips stays stuck. No rough and tumble hound he. I always wonder how he'd lasted on the streets for even one day. But then refusing to go where we want involves sitting too. It's no great challenge to determine this motivation. If he immediately gets up when I agree to go in a different direction than I've just tried, it means he simply has other plans. Then I have to give him a tug, never something I like.

If Sam and I walk him together, we now have another technique – I simply go off in the direction we need Chips to go. Sam stands with Chips, knowing our dog never lets me out of his sight. Sure enough, within a short time, he gets up and follows me, trying to catch up. Even after he's seen this ploy over and over, and no matter how much he wants to go somewhere else, Chips never fails to follow me. In time I feel guilty using his emotional attachment, but not too guilty to use it instead of carrying him. Sometimes while walking away, I turn around to welcome Chips in my direction. And after doing this for a while, it takes longer and longer for him to fall for it. Sam sometimes calls after me, "Don't turn around." And I don't. And Chips always comes.

Just to complete the family profile, my own back problems worsen. As Sam heals, I begin the inevitable visits to Dr. Goldstein, and discover, after my own MRI, that I have a couple of herniated discs and arthritic facet joints, at the very least. Arthritic?! I thought that was only for old people. Rounds of physical therapy, anti-inflammatories and epidurals follow. Also a new bed. Sam and I buy a Tempurpedic, which we figure can only help all of our backs. With the bed frame height, the thicker mattress and base, the new bed is extremely high. Chips has problems jumping on it. He can barely make it, and only with great difficulty. Naturally, we remove the bed frame and skirt which covers the base, to place the bed on the floor. With an ottoman moved from the corner chair and placed in front of our bed, the prince of the castle can now more easily reach the new bed. So much for nighttime adjustments.

Daytime adjustments also need to be made. For obvious reasons, Dr. Goldstein doesn't want me carrying Chips. "Why don't you get a wagon for him" my brother suggests. Not a bad thought. We buy a wagon, but it makes a racket on the street when we pull it along.

"A foldable stroller might be easier to cart around," I tell Sam, "and could definitely help save what's left of our backs." At this time fancy dog strollers had not yet hit the market, so a baby stroller would have to do. We go stroller shopping at ToysRUs. There, along with all the new and expectant mothers, we examine various options for our boy. "How big is your baby," one woman asks me.

"Twenty-six pounds."

"He is a big boy!" I just smile while we settle on a popular, light, inexpensive, easy to fold stroller. I lift Chips into it. He doesn't seem to mind, and could sit on the seat if we put the back all the way down. This requires using a razor to slit open the material that holds the back at an angle.

We start taking the stroller and a towel to line it in the car trunk, especially when we want to have a longer walk than Chips can manage. When he's tired, he slows down, then sits and looks at us. Because I'm better at the proper bended knee technique for lifting, as instructed by Dr. Goldstein, I pick him up and carefully place him in the stroller. It must not be that easy for him to sit all the time it takes us to walk him back to the car. Lying down is a more relaxing and natural position for a dog, so this stroller thing isn't the luxury it seems to be. Nonetheless, it allows the three of us to go for longer walks, especially on weekends. Then there's time to stop for coffee downtown before walking the mile or so back to Sunset Boulevard, where we usually leave our car. But, oh, the comments and looks we get!

As people pass us in cars, they point and laugh. I can just imagine the remarks about pampered Beverly Hills pets going on inside. It reminds us of the joke about the rich woman who comes to the Beverly Hills Hotel in a limo, with lots of luggage and her ten-year-old son. She asks the valets to please carry all the suitcases and her son into the hotel. She overhears one valet whisper to the other, "I guess he can't walk." The woman immediately snaps, "Of course he can, but thank God he doesn't have to!"

If people out walking pass Chips in his stroller, some inevitably comment, "That's the way to go," "What a life," or "talk about spoiled!" A couple of times I see tourists snapping pictures of us. Their attitudes, to be expected, don't bother us a bit. We know what we have to do for Chips. Anyway, being in "the business" in Hollywood, prepares one for any amount of derision.

Chapter 22

AUNT BERTA AND
THE DANCE POLICE

No one...appreciates the very special genius of your conversation as a dog does.

CHRISTOPHER MORLEY

Sam and I used to enjoy dancing at home. If there was a danceable tune on the radio or CD playing, we were used to getting up and making fools of ourselves whenever possible. But shortly after we adopted Chips those days drifted away. This dog had no intention of being left out of any fun. My reading revealed that Tibetans were definitely people dogs and want to be included in whatever the family did. Dogs in general are like that, but Tibetans more insistent.

Whenever Sam and I tried to dance, Chips, true to breed, made his feelings known by jumping on our legs, begging to join in. Not wanting to discourage his growing assertiveness, one or the other of us began, those first months we had him, to pick him up, and hold him between us as we whirled around to the beat. "O.K. Chips, you want to dance?" Sure, it took away from our style some, but, more importantly, Chips loved being held and swung around. He actually smiled. There's an open-mouthed contented look simultaneous with a sparkle in the eyes that's an unmistakable dog smile. People who live with dogs recognize this. And what better feeling can there be than making your dog sublimely happy? We carried on like this for a few years.

Eventually, Sam and, I unable to pick up Chips' twenty-five pound bulk easily, had to give this up. "Avoid heavy lifting," Dr. Goldstein told us. "That means anything over ten pounds." Well, that certainly included Chips. So, when Sam and I had the nerve to try dancing without him, Chips jumped on us and barked, wanting to be included, as in pre-surgery days. But that was no longer possible. Rather than drive our dog nuts or put him out of the room, we just stopped dancing at home, saving our moves on the dance floor for places and events outside the house. Though these times are few and far between, they're worth waiting for so as not to drive Chips crazy. Yes, of course, we make some sacrifices to promote his good feelings but isn't it the same with kids?

The rewards outweigh the deficits. For instance, it's hard to be lonely with a dog around. The feelings of intimacy, and harmony between our species, and a sense of living in the present, pervades. Isn't the emphasis on the moment at hand something all the spiritual gurus and books on happiness remind us to do?

The night before we leave on trips, Aunt Berta always sleeps at our house. She once witnesses this dance routine – our trying and Chips ending our efforts, all within twenty seconds. She couldn't believe how he would not let us dance. She's still the only person we trust to stay with Chips. She's had a difficult life, laced with tragedy. Nonetheless, she's always a caretaker par excellence. If someone in the family became ill, Berta was always there to help him or her.

Years after the family moved to the U.S. in '51, her only brother remaining in Cuba was terminally ill. Berta returned to nurse him, even though Castro was then closing the island for emigration. While hoards of people were leaving Cuba, Berta was the only one on the plane going back. And, sure enough, she got stuck there for five years.

Much later, in the U.S., Berta also took wonderful care of her father and mother before they died. She's a warm and kindly woman, but animals were not on her radar screen. She'd never lived with a pet, and certainly had never gotten close to someone else's. Sam suggested Berta for that first brief stay with Chips because he knew she was completely trustworthy and would follow instructions. But after that, she seemed increasingly impressed by Chips' warmth, sweetness and, I suspect, the fact that he was so good about his bathroom habits. Other dogs she knew about had the occasional or frequent accident, but not Chips. When he needed to go between walks he'd just trot around near you to get your attention, then lead you to the garden door.

Berta never spoke to Chips in English, yet he seemed to understand whatever she said to him in Spanish. Who knew what things they were discussing? Maybe her moving into a building that allowed animals? Whatever it was, she thought he was a genius for understanding it. At least he'd respond to her requests. She grew fonder and fonder of him, as he did of her. When I say "Aunt Berta's coming," he gets excited and runs to the dining room window to look for her. When she arrives, he barks and jumps around, clearly delighted at the prospect of her visit. An added bonus is Berta's generosity with her food. She often brings a turkey sandwich to eat. Turkey is Chips' absolute favorite food. As unwilling to say no to him as we are, Berta enjoys sharing her sandwiches with him. This no doubt enhances her already tremendous appeal.

Berta takes her job as Chips' parent in loci quite seriously. She not only cooks for him, brushes him and takes over the paw washing, but she seeks to reassure him emotionally with a lot of petting and a loving tone of voice. My suggestion to try "baby talk" that first time must have stuck with her because she talks to him just the way a doting Spanish parent or grandparent would to someone under two years old.

One thing bothers us. When we're away on vacation, Berta refuses to leave our house. Even though her sister and nearby brother always offer to pick her up and take her places, because she doesn't drive, she adamantly refuses. Naturally, we feel guilty.

We explain that Chips spends time alone when <u>we</u> need to go somewhere without him, but she simply won't entertain the idea of leaving Chips alone when his parents are away. Not even for an hour! So if we travel for two weeks, that's how long Berta stays in our house without leaving. Unbelievable but true. Imagine this dog's magnetic powers. Chips at least gets to leave for short periods of time with his walkers. But Berta will not. Her sister, brother or granddaughter may visit her and Chips at our house if they like, but she stays put. Is it any wonder that Chips becomes mad about her? At least on Mother's day and birthdays, he never forgets his Aunt.

Chapter 23

GOING, GOING, NOT GOING

A man may smile and bid you hail
Yet wish you to the devil;
But when a good dog wags his tail,
You know he's on the level.

AUTHOR UNKNOWN

Being without kids and having definite wanderlust, Sam and I are perfect candidates for extensive travel. We love to explore new places, but don't want to leave Chips behind too often. Sam tells me that he used take Daisy along when he traveled by plane. She had been exactly twelve pounds. After take-off on flights, she was allowed to join her humans on an empty seat or on their laps. But times have changed dramatically, even for lightweight dogs. Now they have to stay in their carrying cases for takeoff and landing and, depending on the airline attendants, sometimes during the entire flight. The airlines' new strictness followed after 9/11. But it's not easy for dogs to remain in these cases for many hours of travel.

The larger dogs have to go in cargo, in their own kennels. Chips, sensitive and fearful of odd places and noises, would freak out in those areas of the plane. Being alone or with other frightened comrades there would make it a terrifying experience. Also, the conditions – questionable temperature control and noise, make these cargo areas even more uncomfortable for animals. We've heard several horror stories about sick, injured, even dead dogs who had traveled in cargo. Clearly not a good choice for Chips. For the record, there are others who've done this and had no problems.

We know many, many dog parents who'd be willing to pay a hefty premium to be able to take their dogs on a plane. The airlines miss a golden opportunity to make a lot more money than they do. If they offered even a couple of flights a week on frequently traveled routes that allowed dogs in the passenger areas, it would be immensely profitable. Finally, we heard of one airline founded especially for that purpose.

Companion Air, an incipient company, posted its progress to get established on the internet. At least a dozen people we knew were excited about the prospect that at last someone would be doing something to fill this obvious need. Not cheap, it at least would offer some hope of transporting one's dog cross country by air. The airline intended to launch the following year and would offer service only on turboprops. There would be only one class, with compartments for dogs and seats for people in the same passenger area of the plane. No jets, these planes required several flights to actually get cross country. But people will go to a lot of trouble to travel with their pets. We feel Companion Air has the potential of real success. Direct flights on jets, of course, would be more attractive.

After several years of encouraging postings with indicated delays, the enterprise apparently folded without ever getting off the ground either literally or figuratively. Disappointing to say the least. But in a country with so many entrepreneurs and animal lovers, I have no doubt that someone will one day fill this need. In the meantime, we have no way to take Chips with us when we travel by plane to see family or friends in the U.S.

Our trips once or twice a year are never more than two weeks. But that's a long time for Chips to be without us. And finding trustworthy walkers is a dicey project. At least a dozen terrible things can happen on walks -– dog or coyote attacks, broken glass on the street, car accidents that spill over onto the sidewalk. The person has to be responsible, as well as kind and smart. We're lucky to have found a few people we could trust, but they weren't always available. None of them lived in Beverly Hills, so they had to drive here from wherever – usually pretty far – make their way up the hill, put Chips in the car and drive down to the flats. Then the walk would begin. Afterwards, he'd have to be put back in the car and driven home again. We worried about how Chips would jump in and out of cars with high seats. Some of the walkers had SUVs. After Chips' back trouble began, this became a larger issue.

Through the years, we and Berta go through many anxious times with walkers. One doesn't show up. When I reach him the next day, he admits, "I had a fight with my girlfriend and just forgot." Another one phones me in Positano, on the Amalfi Coast, and says "I have to finish writing a play and just don't have time for this." That from a friend of mine who'd asked me several times for the job. Of course making alternate arrangements from Italy proved difficult, but not impossible.

Sam, never at ease when away from Chips, worries enough for both of us; he calls home to check on our boy's well being from wherever we are in the world. The calls are at first placed every five days or so, but as the years go by, they became more and more frequent. After Chips turns nine, Sam calls every day. Whether we're in Turkey, Tahiti or New York, the phone company can count on at least one call a day from Sam to his sister for reassurance of Chips' well being.

One year we are planning a trip to Crete to visit friends for the opening of their new home there. We ask Berta if she's available to stay with our boy. She is. We're excited about the trip and book flights. But as the months passed it's <u>my</u> back this time that gets worse and worse. "It seems this back thing is contagious" I tell Sam. We think twice about the trip.

Chapter 24

BY THE BEAUTIFUL SEA

When you love a dog and it loves you, the lack of synchronization between human and animal life is bound to bring sorrow.

ROGER GRENIER

After cancelling our flights to Crete, we spend most of the summer of '06 in Carmel I've sold the movie rights to my first book, after having had six development deals on it. Sometimes the winds of Hollywood blow in the direction of the most persistent. However, not all is well – <u>my</u> back worsens by the day. I can only walk a few blocks, in significant pain, before needing to rest. Now Sam and I must take Chips out together on the path above the ocean. When I need to stop on a bench or large rock to recuperate, Sam walks on with Chips. Often, though, Chips rests with me. Once in a while, he still whimpers near the staircase while watching others romping on the beach and running in the water. But between greeting his canine and human friends on the path, visiting Diggedy Dog and sitting in the stroller when he grows weak, he still manages to have pretty pleasant jaunts.

During July, I realize that a much smaller, sparsely populated beach in Pebble Beach, next to Carmel, allows dogs off leash. There are only a few very wide steps that go down to the sand. I wonder if Chips can manage going up them without assistance. As we walk close to the area he begins sniffing the air. Obviously, he wants to go closer to the water. I step onto the first large, flat stair with him straining in his harness. I check the beach, named Stillwater Cove, to make sure no dogs I don't know are there. "I don't want any trouble, Chips." All clear. I take off his leash. Before I reach the bottom stair my boy's dashing down the sand, ears flying back in the wind. He's actually having a great time again.

Having only seen him like this rarely, I'm thrilled as I watch him barking at the small waves, running and intermittently stopping to sniff seaweed or pee on rocks. Suddenly a small dog, maybe a Jack Russell, appears out of nowhere and runs over to Chips. He seems aggressive; I hurry over to them. The dog actually bites Chips on the face, but not enough to draw blood. I get between them as Chips shakes his head and touches his paw to his cheek. Forget my back – I swoop down to lift him out of the smaller dog's reach. "Your dog bit him" I say to the totally unconcerned old woman who walks behind the smaller dog, She ignores me and keeps walking with her dog.

Another woman, walking toward us, has seen what happened. "That dog has bitten so many dogs," she says. "The woman used to live in that house" she continues, pointing to a Pebble Beach mansion facing the ocean behind the famous golf course, "but since being divorced she no longer lives here and is extremely bitter." Everyone has a story.

After that first encounter with the Jack Russell, I see the same dog repeatedly in the Pebble Beach area, always off his leash, even when not on the beach. I make sure to put myself between Chips and the other dog. I shoo him away when he comes close. Only once, at the end of the summer, does the woman finally put a leash on her dog. I hadn't said a word to her since the day of the bite, but when she finally did it I said, "Thank you."

Chips and I repeat the visits to Stillwater Cove many times that summer, but I always check first to make sure that the biter is nowhere in sight. Usually, he isn't, and Chips gets his visit. We're both happy, especially after he makes friends with the Harbor Master. A fellow who directs the small boats from the pier, his station is a little hut at the end of it. Chips discovers that the man has a box of dog cookies, which he offers a few of to Chips. After that there's no stopping my boy from heading down the pier whenever he visits Stillwater Cover. The weeks wear on. Chips manages to have a good summer, but I walk shorter and shorter distances before my back pain stops me. All the medical opinions I seek agree – I need a fusion of the L5 and S1 vertabrae because one vertebra is significantly out of line.

When we return to L.A. with a new x-ray, I take it to Dr. Goldstein. He also concurs that after eight and a half years of trying everything else to help my problem, no alternative to surgery remains. I know that Dr. Goldstein is the surgeon I want. He feels confident that the fusion will work, and I trust his skill. Naturally, Chips needs to be taken care of during my hospital stay so that Sam's free to visit with me. Once again we enlist Berta's reliable assistance. When I return home from the hospital, Dr. Chips helps all he can by sticking next me whenever he's not eating or walking. His constant affectionate presence along with Sam's superb care hasten my complete recovery.

The healing qualities of dogs, and no doubt some husbands, have been well documented. Nursing homes with dogs or cats living there report a sharp decrease in medication needed by the residents. In fact, pet parents in general are reputed to have better health. Responsibility for a pet also helps people recuperate from illness, if only because the guardians know that the pets are dependent upon them for their care. Perhaps it also distracts them from their own problems. Whatever Chips does for the two of us, it has worked.

On the first day Chips, Sam and I can go for a walk together I feel triumphant. Although Sam holds the leash, we are all actually doing something other than waiting for me to heal. After a few more months, I go back to walking Chips alone most of the time. If I ever accidentally drop the leash, he immediately stops, waiting for me to pick it up. Maybe he senses that I cannot run after him. I'm sure he wouldn't have done this in his youth, but by now his need to run is gone, and he must feel that we're connected in some powerful way. I know I do. Each of us being on opposite ends of the leash symbolizes his sense of security and my sense of belonging with him. We're one – the leash just being the material display. I like being part of Chips. The feeling of belonging to and with him provides a comfort known to many dog "owners".

Sam and I begin making plans to go to Crete again the following late spring. Would we finally make it?

Chapter 25

THE PSYCHIC
AND THE CONVICT

I am his Highness dog at Kew
Pray tell me, sir, whose dog are you?

ON THE COLLAR OF A DOG

(IMITATIONS OF HORACE, EPISTLE 1)

One of the things we enjoy with our social boy is taking him with us to outdoor restaurants. In Carmel, any restaurant with outdoor tables welcome dogs. Many similar places in Los Angeles do not. There used to be more of them, but in recent years they've gotten less dog friendly. Apparently, the Los Angeles Health Department has a rule that dogs "cannot be in the food area," but no definition is provided to indicate

251

whether this means inside, outside, where food is prepared or anything more specific. Our experience is that some restaurants interpret "food area" as anywhere food is served, including tables on the sidewalk. Some restaurants don't do this. Many, many restaurant owners tell us that they've been hassled by health inspectors, so they can't welcome dogs anymore. Others don't seem to have a problem.

Needless to say, our preferred restaurants and those of our dog owning friends, are the welcoming kind. The whole idea that people who have pets in their homes with food and kitchens cannot control them in restaurants seems silly. The folks who came up with these laws should take a trip to France and see the dogs curled up comfortably under the tables inside the finest restaurants. Apparently no problems have arisen to make the French change their laws. But in Beverly Hills, life is not that easy. If you're walking your dog and happen to get hungry, you'd better be near a dog friendly establishment or forget eating with the pooch.

Leaving a dog tied up outside on the sidewalk is not something we'd ever consider. Besides feeling scared and lonely, the dog can get stepped on, dognapped, teased or touched by kids in an inappropriate manner. So when a decent restaurant welcomes dogs, it tends to always be full. We go again and again to those places. One memorable, sunny and warm December day we order lunch at just such a popular restaurant. I take out Chips' dog treats when a middle aged woman lunching at a nearby table, walks over. "Excuse me for interrupting you, but I'm psychic, and I'm getting very strong vibrations from your dog."

"Uh huh." To have someone say this in Los Angeles is nothing remarkable. But I don't think that in all parts of this country or in other countries the statement would be met with the same equanimity. Doubtless, Sam is as surprised and interested as I am.

"Would you like to know more about his background" she continues. Somehow the woman knows that we're completely in the dark about Chips' early years.

"Sure."

"Well, he was originally owned by an older lady. Things were o.k. until the woman got sick and had to bring in a caretaker. This caretaker used to place your dog in a corner and tell him to stay there. She was very strict with him. After the owner died, there were many people coming in and going out of the house. This dog, who was no longer happy there, slipped out and ran away."

While the woman petted Chips we thanked her for the information and confirmed that he hadn't been with us for his whole life. Then she went back to her table. It was an isolated incident that changed nothing – an L.A. moment. We would never know whether or not the information was true, but no doubt the woman believed it. Later that night we have a talk with Chips, who does nothing to deny her story.

At the same restaurant where the psychic hangs out, on another day, Sam, his brother, Ruben, Chips and I sit eating breakfast at an outside table with my chair closest to the street. Chips is lying at my feet when another customer, a middle aged man, jumps up and begins running toward his parked car. It seems he spotted a meter maid near his vehicle and wanted to avoid a ticket. As he runs by Chips, he seems to either hit his tail or foot. Suddenly, Chips jumps up on the man's leg for a second as the guy goes by. When he returns the man says "Your dog bit me." I'm completely dumbstruck. Chips is about nine at this time and has never bitten anyone.

"Are you sure?"

The guy points to a barely visible tear in his chinos pant leg, yelling "And, lady, you just bought these pants. They were one hundred seventy-five dollars at

Bergdorf's." Now I know that Bergdorf Goodman is expensive, but I'd personally never seen chinos for one hundred seventy-five. However, that's not the issue. As the guy stands menacingly over Chips, he strikes terror in this mother's heart – I fear that the guy might become violent toward our boy. "And he better have his rabies shot!" the man fumes.

"Oh, he has. We'll be happy to send you a copy of the certificate," I tell him, still doubting that Chips has bitten him. Meanwhile, knowing L.A. to be the capital of frivolous lawsuits, Sam whips out his wallet and, fortunately, has exactly $175.00. Giving it to the guy, hoping this will placate him, he apologizes for any harm that Chips might have done him. "He's never bitten anyone," I tell the man "...and he's always been incredibly friendly." But the guy by now has worked himself up into an angry frenzy, almost frothing at the mouth as he laments his ruined breakfast.

I turn to reassuring Chips who looks disturbed about the commotion while Sam commiserates with the guy. The fellow lifts his pants leg. Sam tells me that he does have a small scratch, but no bite marks or blood. Perhaps it was Chips' nail or a tooth. I get this information later from Sam, but I never see the damage. Still, we exchange names, addresses and phone

numbers. Again reassuring the man that we'll immediately send him a copy of the rabies certificate, all of
us go back to eating our breakfasts. That seems to
be the end of the problem. In short order, we get the
check and pay it, anxious to be away from "the scene
of the crime."

We aren't halfway down the block when a police-
man stops us. Out of the corner of my eye I spot what
looks like an animal control truck across the street.
Incredibly to us, the guy called the cops! Talk about
sangfroid. I had visions of my baby being dragged
into a truck and off to doggie prison. We tell the
officer the entire story. The cop looks at our identifi-
cation, actually pets Chips and seems sympathetic to
our situation. "I have no choice except to give you a
citation. Animal Control will contact you." Sam and
I are stunned. "But I can get your $175.00 back, if you
want."

"No, thanks," Sam says, not wanting to do anything
to inflame the already emotional guy. Disbelieving
and depressed about what's happened, Sam, Ruben
and I walk the few blocks to Ruben's house. We talk
about what might take place next. We're all very upset
about the consequences of this run-in with the law.
"He'll probably sue us for God knows what," Sam wor-

ries. I wonder, would someone try to take Chips somewhere terrible?

In Ruben's living room, we speculate about several dire scenarios, then drive home, close the front curtains, go into the small back room and talk in hushed voices about what action we might take if anyone tries to take Chips from us. "We could move to Canada," I suggest. Sam vaguely nods. No doubt we won't let ourselves be separated from Chips. Though we don't think it's all right for dogs to bite people, this was hardly a vicious dog in attack mode. It's an isolated reaction to a surprise attack on a foot or tail.

"Imagine him being back at a pound or worse without us," Sam thinks aloud. "He goes into a funk if we leave him to go to a movie." His mental meltdown would be too awful to contemplate. If that threat becomes real we will obviously have to run away with him, become fugitives from the law. We reassure each other that paying whatever the price of keeping him with us would be worth it. This trauma calls for a consultation with Nancy. Seven dogs of her own must have provided her with the every permutation of existing dog problems.

"Chips won't be taken away, but will probably be confined to your house for ten days," she tells us. "The animal control people will also come and check that he's there a few times. Also, you'll have to show his rabies certificate." I couldn't believe it. My blood begins to unfreeze as I tell Sam the somewhat good news.

"No one's going to take our boy away." But Sam's still upset about anyone having it in for Chips, who by now has picked up our anxiety. He paces back and forth while Sam and I discuss how best to proceed. I decide to phone Animal Control and speak of "a friend" with our situation and ask "what would she have to do?"

The officer who answers tells me, "She'd have to come down to Carson with the dog's license and rabies certificate, and fill out some papers." That doesn't sound too bad. We decide to go right away and leave Chips at home, lest anyone at the shelter wants to snatch him from us. We feel sure that no one would break into our house to do so.

Our nerves still on edge, we drive forty-five minutes to the animal control center and shelter in Carson. There, we give our information, show Chips' rabies certificate, and answer all the questions for their report. They already have the citation in their computers. Quite an efficient system when it comes to tracking indicted dogs. Too bad human animal abusers don't feel the hand of the law that quickly. If only dogs who are bitten or abused got the kind of protection the law gives to people no matter how minor their injuries, the world would be a better place.

Sam speaks Spanish with the personnel there; a definite rapport develops among them. After chatting with Sam for a while, one of the men actually asks him to have lunch with him to discuss "his career and possible moves." Sam, need I say, only too gladly agrees to do so. We aren't able to make a contribution to a college to get Chips in, but this was the least we could do to help keep him out of a penitentiary.

We're told, as Nancy accurately predicted, to confine Chips at home for ten days. I do not understand how this house arrest serves anyone. It's certainly no pleasure for the dog. There's zero benefit for the person who was "bitten." And once the dog's proven not to carry rabies, what is the point? Ten days can be an eternity for a dog. Chips is used to at least two walks a day, in addition to accompanying me on most errands and shopping trips. The physical therapy place I go to for my back even welcomes him. He's so eager to go along whenever I leave the house that I know he'll be really downhearted at not going out.

Our plan to evade the law is hatched that night in the dark. For two law abiding citizens, actually members of the Community Emergency Response Team, it may seem out of character, but, yes, I must confess that we planned on violating Chips' parole. It had to be done carefully. We assume that checking up on him would take place during normal working hours or close to them. Therefore, if we want to give our dog a walk it has to be before or after that time. And just in case he's spotted by someone who recognizes him in Beverly Hills we decide to drive to another neighborhood. The idea that the local police were cruising around with Chips' mug shot taped to their dashboard could not be dismissed. After all, the B.H. police, compared to those in other cities, have relatively few crimes to deal with.

The next morning we get up by alarm before dawn, jump – okay, drag, into our sweats and drive stealthily away in Sam's old sports car. I feel like a druggie heading in cover of darkness to meet my dealer. We make poor Chips sit on the floor, in the foot well of the small car so that he can't be seen, and facing me so there is at least something to look at. No doubt he wonders why, after always riding in the little space behind the seats, or on my lap, he's suddenly consigned to riding backwards on the floor. But dogs always have to go along with the nutty behavior of their people. I'm sure he doesn't understand this or a myriad of other things that we request of him.

Nervously, we drive to Holmby Hills, a ten minute ride West on Sunset Boulevard. There we walk our boy in a lovely park just as the light begins to show. Chips, blissfully unaware that he's become a fugitive from the law, sniffs butts, lifts leg and generally does all he wants. By the time the sun really shines we're already home. The whole process gets repeated every dawn and dusk for ten days. Chips' entire parole period at least affords him two outings a day. In between, he simply has to stay at home. Feeling sorry that he can't come out on my errands, I buy him a CD to keep him company when I'm gone.

"Mozart For Dogs" comes to my attention in some dog catalogue. It says "music that enhances the lives of our best friends." Who knew the musical prodigy was a dog lover? O.K. I don't actually believe that Mozart wrote this specifically for dogs. I assume that the people selling the CDs have done some research to backup their assumptions. I buy and put it on with great anticipation. If our dog likes regular classical music, imagine how thrilled he'd be with pieces manipulated to be particularly good for dogs. The music begins playing. It's just a normal piece of music – nothing added. Chips remains completely under-whelmed.

I thought they'd actually have used Mozart as a basis for some psychically enhanced music. Another silly purchase, I muse. How in the world could anyone know what pieces by Mozart any dog would prefer? But I had to hand it to the folks who market this stuff – if enough fools like me fall for the title, they can make some good money. By the way, the same company also has "Beethoven For Cats." Why don't I put out Puccini for Parrots or Tchaikowsky for Turtles? But then I'm not in that business.

During the ten days of Chips' confinement we receive notices that the animal control people came by several times and saw Chips in the window barking. Though Sam and I fear being discovered breaking the law, we get through it without mishap. But we'd like to go on record with this confession to say that we have not committed any more criminal acts since. How-ever, if Chips again needed our help..........

Chapter 26

SHOCK WAVES

Dogs teach us an important lesson by easily adapting to the changing circumstances of life.

THE MONKS OF NEW SKETE

By the time Chips has been with us ten years, he needs his teeth cleaned again. We take him to the vet where we also plan to have a growth on his stomach removed under general anesthesia. The last time they'd cleaned his teeth, the then tiny growth had gotten overlooked. Now it was a good deal larger. Dr. Olds tells us, "Because Chips is around twelve years old, the protocol is to do a blood test first to see if he can withstand the anesthesia." I feel positive all will be fine. Chips' youthful spirit and good health are evident.

"The liver function seems to be off" Dr. Olds says when the blood test comes back. "We could do a liver panel to find out more." Without any doubt, we want that done. A few days later, the results of the new tests come in. They don't sound good. We talk to Dr. Martin, Chips' internist, about the possible causes. There's Cushings Disease, something our friends' dog once had. "But Chips doesn't really display any of the symptoms for the illness," he tells us. "We can do an ultrasound of the liver to see if anything more shows." We agree to the ultrasound. The radiologist will be there a few days later.

Sam and I are naturally our usual anxious selves. However, Chips still seems as bouncy as always, tail constantly wagging, so that we're hopeful it won't be anything too serious. The ultrasound presents one difficulty – they have to shave Chips' belly area. Of course we need to muzzle him as he isn't about to stand still for someone shaving and doing strange things to his belly. This would be a much longer time than he's ever muzzled before. The whole business takes about a half hour.

When the Doctor's through we go in for the results. Dr. Martin shows us the film. "I'm afraid it's a liver tumor," he says pointing it out. I can't believe it. My beloved brother, Ralph, had died of a liver tumor seven years before this. He was someone who looked and felt in perfect health until he began to have symptoms, got checked and discovered a grapefruit sized tumor that was wrapped around the portal vein of his liver. Despite all efforts, he passed away a brief six weeks later. The words "liver tumor" struck panic into my heart.

The mass seems to be confined to one area or lobe. "The dog's liver," Dr. Martin explains, "has six lobes. Perhaps the tumor is benign. No metastasis can be seen." Though an encouraging note, the idea that Chips might have a malignant tumor would have to be faced. Subconsciously, Sam and I both assumed that a very well cared for dog of this long lived breed could be with us for many more years. After all, he'd had wonderful veterinary attention, been given the best food we could offer, and seemed incredibly youthful for his age. People always mistook him for a very young dog. With a tail that wagged incessantly, Chips seemed a sure candidate for longevity. "Given the size of the tumor," Dr. Martin continues, "it's best to come out, even if it is benign. Left in, the tumor will eventually affect the liver function."

We talk with Dr. Olds, about doing a biopsy, but decide we don't want Chips to go through that, then have to endure another procedure with anesthesia. We'd do both the biopsy and operation at once. Driving home from the vet, Sam and I remain sad and shaken. We talk some more about it that night, then decide it's pointless to put off the inevitable. We call the next day to set a date for surgery. It would take place the following week.

In the meantime, the idea of possibly losing Chips in an untimely manner weighs on us heavily even as we watch our healthy looking dog enjoying life. Now every day he's with us becomes even more precious than it was before. Just in case the tumor turns out to be malignant we talk about oncologists to our friend Marjorie, who works at the same clinic where we go. She strongly recommends a new state of the art oncology center in Culver City, twenty minutes from where we live. Her own cat is being treated there. We make an appointment at the City of Angels oncology center for a date ten days after Chips' surgery, just in case the tumor is malignant.

Neither Sam nor I sleep the night before Chips' operation. This had to be taken quite seriously. We know we might possibly lose him, but try to think positively. "Chips is otherwise healthy," I say. And we have complete confidence in Dr. Olds.

"Maybe we should have gone up to Davis, where they have state of the art equipment" Sam thinks out loud. Davis is the veterinary college where we'd gone once before. We loved our surgeon, but was his operating room up to snuff? We don't know.

Chips' favorite bowl is the one we keep upstairs in the bedroom for his water. For whatever reason, he prefers the smallish pottery bowl, that had once belonged to Sam's Daisy, to his larger one downstairs. That night we have to take it away as he's not allowed to eat or drink for eight hours before anesthesia. Here we were again, another awful night before a trauma for Chips.

Early the next morning, we deliver our little guy to the clinic. Dr. Olds greets us in his surgical hat and gown. Chips would be his first surgery. "I'll call you as soon as I'm done," he assures us. We give him our cell phone numbers and tell him we'll be around the corner at the coffee shop.

About midway through our breakfast, my cell phone rings. "It's Dr. Olds."

I stop breathing when I hear his voice. It's much too soon for the operation to be over. Did something go wrong? My heart is in my throat. I can't say a word. "The tumor is much deeper than it looked on the ultrasound. I even tried pulling on it but couldn't get it out. I could certainly remove it by cutting a lot deeper. But it's higher risk. I'm not sure what you'd like me to do." The message was clear – "higher risk" meant that Chips had an increased chance of dying on the table.

"One moment please." I repeat to Sam what Dr. Olds has told me. It takes about ten seconds for Sam and I to agree to have him just close Chips up. Our reasoning is that we are not prepared to lose our wonderful dog right then. We feel that his small body could take only so much punishment. More significantly, he has no symptoms. That means that for the moment at least he is enjoying life. We want that to continue for as long as possible. And the tumor might be benign. When Chips' pleasures diminish and suffering begins, we would, understandably, do what we had to.

"No, we don't want to take the higher risk. Just do the biopsy and close him up because he has no symptoms."

"O.K. I think that's right. He looks great now. Sometimes later, when the tumor is bigger, it's often easier to get out." I hang up. Sam has tears in his eyes. I dissolve after looking at him. We hold hands over our uneaten breakfast and review our decision. No matter what the biopsy shows, we feel it's the right choice for now.

"I told you he was a poor little guy," Sam whispers. I nod in agreement.

"Right now he's not suffering. When that happens we'll know what to do." We push the food away. After sitting there another few minutes, we walk slowly back to the clinic.

A short time later Dr. Olds comes out to the waiting room. "I would have done the same thing you did." That definitely makes us feel better.

"He's so well now," I manage.

"Exactly. And we might get it out later, as I mentioned. You want to see him?" He takes us in to where Chips lies still unconscious on a towel in a room adjacent to the operating room.

"Make sure he has all the pain medication he needs," Sam tells the Doctor.

"Of course. The biopsy should come back in a few days. You can pick him up tomorrow morning." We drive home, reviewing our decision, hoping that we've made the right choice. There's no doubt that we're disappointed the tumor hasn't been removed. The idea of it being too difficult to get out never crossed our minds.

The next morning a tail wagging, "smiling" Chips on his own four feet greets us in Dr. Olds' office. His appearance definitely lifts our spirits. Dr. Olds also smiles as he hands me his leash. "You did the right thing. Just look at him. We'll call you in a few days when the biopsy results come back."

Outside we open the back door of the car; Chips tries to jump in. He yelps painfully and falls back. That cry tears through us. I bend down to pick him up, being careful not to touch his stomach area but rather put one arm under his chest and another under his hind legs and tail, the way I'd seen the technicians do. My back was healed. If I used the proper bended knee technique that Dr. Goldstein showed me, I'd be all right.

"I'm afraid it's malignant," Dr. Martin tells us a few days later. He hands us a report which states that Chips has an aggressive malignant tumor.

"The majority of hepatocellular carcinomas in the dog do not exhibit distant metastasis until late in the course of the disease. But intrahepatic spread may occur. This neoplasm is cytologially more malignant than most canine hepatocellular carcinomas, but it is not known if this indicates more aggressive biologic behavior." Sounds ominous, especially "more malignant than most."

I know that both Sam and I are thinking of my poor brother, who'd lasted such a short time after his liver tumor was discovered. I gaze down at Chips, innocently wagging his tail, jumping on my legs, reminding me that it's time to get the hell out of there. My little boy would not be with us much longer. "The main thing is we do not want him to suffer at all," I say, knowing Sam feels exactly the same way.

"How will we know if he's suffering?" Sam asks Dr. Martin.

"You will. It'll be obvious. And his eating is a good indication. I've seen some dogs with cancer go quite a long time."

"How long?"

"Hard to say exactly. Just enjoy him." We intend to do just that. As we leave, a pall of gloom descends on us, but seeing Chips' happy face helps us cope with the knowledge of the pain to come. The blessing of being a dog, and there are so few, is that there's an innocence, and an ignorance of the future and death that makes the present much happier. Fortunately, Chips, like all of his kind, live in the moment. Right now, the moment isn't at all bad.

On the way home we talk about what we could do to make sure the last part of Chips' life would be as good as possible. "Spending time with him certainly heads the list." Not knowing how long he has means putting any new travel plans on hold. Whatever cooking for Chips had taken place before would now be ramped up so that he gets only food he really enjoys, especially his favorite things like the dried turkey treats. Sam orders another dozen packages of them, which I think perhaps overly optimistic, but I wasn't going to discourage him from assuming that Chips would live long enough to consume them. I pray that he's right.

Chapter 27

CROSSROADS

*One reason a dog can be such a comfort when
you're feeling blue is that he doesn't
try to figure out why.*

AUTHOR UNKNOWN

Even though the malignant tumor remains in
Chips, we decide to keep our appointment with the
oncologist just in case there's anything more we can
do for our little guy. In the waiting area of City of
Angels veterinary oncology center we watch dogs coming and going from their chemo and radiation treatments. They look O.K. Some people say they would
never do such things to their pets, but we've known
others whose animals have benefitted greatly and

handled the treatments quite well. Some regret doing it. We're open to ideas for improving Chips' situation and prolonging his life, but not at the cost of more suffering.

The oncologist, Dr. Sue Downing, reads the pathology report, then gets down on the floor to examine Chips. She's very gentle and takes her time with us. We explain what happened in the surgery, then ask if there's anything more to be done. "If you did chemo, you'd get maybe an extra few months," she's honest enough to tell us. I like that. I knew that Sam and I feel the same on this – we would not put Chips through any more discomfort without a significant payoff. After all, he wasn't able to choose to go through difficulties in exchange for a little longer on this earth or with loved ones. I again thank God that dogs only live in the present.

"Is there anything else that can be done?" I ask.

"Well, we're just starting to do this procedure where we cut off the blood supply to the tumor." That sounded hopeful to me. I'd seen TV programs on this procedure starting to be done on people. "The doctor who's going to do it will be here in a few weeks. He's coming from Pittsburgh," she said. They hadn't actually performed these surgeries yet.

When Dr. Downing steps out of the room, Sam and I talk about it. Being the first to have some surgical procedure is not a great thing. Sam had been convinced to have a cardio seal placed into his heart to correct a space between the two ventricles. It was a fairly new procedure, which took less than a half hour and sounded quite simple. But actually it triggered many problems after that. We are not anxious for Chips to be a medical pioneer with a new surgery.

"How long does he have if we do nothing," I ask when the Doctor returns.

"Three months to a year." Back on the floor, she's gently massaging Chips' head. "Hard to tell."

"How will we know when things are getting really bad?"

"Vomiting and diarrhea." That sounds awful. I immediately resolve in my mind that I wouldn't let Chips go through any of those symptoms for long. "You'll know," she adds.

"What about pain," Sam asks.

"This isn't really a painful cancer. He should be o.k. until near the end." The Doctor then offers us some liver support powders, in three different jars. We leave with a feeling of consolation that Chips wasn't in pain, and has no knowledge of what is ahead. But we fear the future and the loss we face.

When I get home I look carefully at the powders we've bought, consisting of liver extracts and such. They have a scooper with them. Several scoops of the three different powders are to be placed on Chips' food at least twice a day. That amount of powder would pretty much obscure all his food, both the kibble and the cooked protein I always add to it. The only way I could get him to eat it would be to give him nothing without the powders and force him to consume them in order to eat. That was exactly contrary to what we wanted do for the end of his life.

Giving him more of his favorite foods, chicken, turkey and meat, was our inclination. However, I had just finished reading a book entitled THE CHINA STUDY. It is a very convincing account by a former National Institute of Health physician regarding cancer and animal protein. His conclusion after many years and studies was that the more animal protein in the diet, the more cancer there'd be. In no uncertain terms he was advocating a vegan diet. For that reason and the difficulty of administering these powders to Chips we decide to abandon any liver extracts. Perhaps I was rationalizing the fact that I couldn't see how to give it to him, but the book was quite convincing. Also, at this point I wouldn't go so far as to deny Chips the foods he liked.

A holistic vet, the one we had consulted years ago on Chips' allergies, had kept a friend's Tibetan Terrier going for almost two years after she was diagnosed with cancer. Sam and I thought that perhaps he might offer something herbal to help Chips' immune system. After a visit to him we come away with three more jars of powders, this time Chinese herbs. When we get home and read the directions, the quantities required are again several scoops of each one per day. No way Chips would take those down. After trying them once with the expected results, I put the new powders aside as well. We now had three hundred dollars worth of powders we weren't going to use.

Sam and I resolve that for whatever time Chips has left we would try to have it be the best possible experience for him. Our attention would be more than ever on making him as comfortable and happy as possible. His needs, both emotional and physical were our focus. Though we'd always treated him like the conscious being he obviously was, with similar sensitivities and needs to our own, we double our efforts. We stop what we're doing more often to talk to and touch him for no reason other than affection and recognition. Sometimes, while I'm writing, Chips comes over and just looks at me, wagging his tail, or puts his paws up on my knees. "Are you looking for love in all the right places? The pleasure's all mine." I pick him up and spend a moment hugging, kissing and generally telling him he's numero uno.

Gauging whether or not Chips wants to sleep or be active gets easier. As spring gives way to summer Chips begins some vomiting. I talk to Dr. Martin who thinks that the mostly yellow bile might simply be from reflux, acid created by too many hours with no food. He suggests I give him something easy to digest before bedtime. Chips' new nightly snack becomes cottage cheese mixed with warmed baked potato. The vomiting disappears.

When June rolls around we return to Carmel, realizing that this surely is Chips' last visit here. He still seems pretty spry, but begins having stomach problems. In between not feeling well, he does fine, wagging his tail almost all the time. I think he needs something like white rice to help him along, but it doesn't solve the problem. Again I consult Dr. Martin who tells us, "I think that Chips needs <u>more</u> fiber in his diet, not less." That surprises me. He suggests a high fiber kibble sold only by vets.

As soon as I start Chips on the regimen of the new kibble, mixed with his usual chicken or meat and veggies, his stomach condition improves immediately. However, he grows weaker in general. Some days he takes a while to get out of bed. It's also more difficult for him going up stairs. We increasingly use his stroller during walks.

When visiting Carmel, we always bathe Chips at a pet store in Pacific Grove. They have elevated bathtubs for pooches so that it's a lot easier on the guardians' backs. Home tubs, on the floor or sunken, require a lot more bending and lifting. The elevated tubs have a few large steps going up to them. Strangely enough, although Chips dislikes being wet, he willingly hops up the two big steps here and waits to be lifted into the tub. This is a very short distance to lift him. Even I can do it with no problem.

For Chips, bathing by mom and dad is an unpleasant but preferable option to bathing by a groomer. Despite our full plastic aprons, Sam and I manage to get soaking wet during this process. Once Chips is soaped up he always gives a good shake, spraying us until we're almost as wet as he is. I look at Sam, disheveled and wet, wrist deep in suds and know exactly why I'm so crazy about him.

While paying for Chips' bath and towels, discards from the posh Pebble Beach Club we're told, we chat with the clerk who knows Chips. Mention of his liver cancer prompts her to tell us about a natural compound used by the owner of the store on her Dalmatian with a malignant breast tumor. "The pills arrested the tumor's growth. In fact, they shrunk it completely away." We're eager to read the literature she finds and hands us on this medicine, Artemisinin, developed by two physicians at the University of Washington. I call one of the doctors. He tells me that they've had some wonderful success with several types of cancer, but have not used it on liver cancer.

"Why don't you give it a try?" he suggests. I order the pills from a company in California. After about a week of the one a day regimen, Chips seems a bit more energetic. He starts walking a little longer. One day, I decide to take a chance and let him go to the beach in Carmel, his fondest wish. With his improved strength, I want him to have at least one more fun time there.

We go down the long staircase with little trouble. Sloshing through the soft sand is not easy but at last we reach the harder, wetter, packed sand near the water. Although Chips can't run as he used to, he strolls along without a leash, visiting with other dogs, venturing to the water's edge, having a definite good time. Thinking to preserve what energy he has, I bring a large towel for us to sit on. Naturally, he lays down half off the towel, which ultimately results in a flea bite, but for one glorious hour, we have a perfect beach time together. I take photos of him near the water and assume it will be our last trip there. Getting up the stairs, and back to the street proves difficult going; fortunately, he makes it without help from my now pain free back.

After a few more weeks on the pill, Chips definitely improves. We do all we can with him in this wonderful dog loving town. One afternoon, walking together on the path along the golf course at Pebble Beach, Chips spots the large ducks that daily come out of the water and walk around the course. He immediately goes into stalking mode, eager to get to those smaller animals. Of course he's not allowed on the course. One fellow I meet with his own dog says, "You can let him run after hours when no one is playing."

"Really?" Should I let Chips terrorize some poor waddling ducks? Of course not. The guy saw me glancing at the animals.

"Oh, the ducks take care of themselves" the man says, apparently reading my mind. The next evening, about 7:30, while still light out, Chips gets his chance. I unclip his leash.

"Are you kiddin' me?" his incredulous look seems to say. And he takes off toward the ducks. Stopping several yards away, he assumes his stalking posture, placing one foot at a time carefully after another; immediately the ducks waddle off to the water. Chips runs after them to the water's edge. He stops as they swim away. And eventually the great hunter joins me back on the path to keep walking. We are headed toward the Pebble Beach Lodge, a dog friendly hotel, where he's meeting his two pals, Aspen and Lady Jane, in the lobby. The four legged trio will quench their thirst with filtered water while the two legged group downs stronger stuff.

It's almost the end of summer. We have a trip to Japan scheduled, the plans made long before we knew about Chips' cancer. Now we're too nervous about leaving him, even with Berta. If he suddenly takes a turn for the worse, she wouldn't know how to cope. Also, we don't want to leave him when he needs us most, or give up any precious time we still have left together. We assume that the cancellation insurance we'd purchased for the trip would reimburse us for our deposit. But upon cancelling we discover that the insurance is only for medical crises and conditions concerning humans, not animals. We aren't able to get our deposit back. But the consolation is that Chips still fares quite well.

We return to Los Angeles, continue the Artemisinin and the high fiber food, but notice that he isn't really crazy about the kibble anymore. But with his stomach stable now and all going along smoothly, we don't want to take him off what works so well. I'm really conflicted – do what's good for him or just what he wants.

Chapter 28

HOLDING ON

---

*The more I see of the representatives of the people,
the more I admire my dogs.*

FROM COUNT D'ORSAY, LETTER TO JOHN FORSTER

In the Fall of '07 I'm working on a new script, but
devote fewer hours to it than to the care and feeding
of Chips, my first priority. Many people, seeing me
out with him, pushing the empty stroller along, ask
"Where's the baby?" When I point to Chips, walking
beside it, and explain that he isn't well, they find it
hard to believe. His bouncy walk, the one he's always
had, and lively personality seem to send a good health
message that makes us feel the decision not to remove
the tumor was probably right.

During outings all together in the car, when Sam drives, I begin riding in the back seat next to Chips, resting my arm on the side of his bed, recently placed there to stabilize his ride. After we'd been rear ended again at a red light, he'd fallen off the back seat. The bed at least now holds him in place. Also, Chips likes the closeness and frequent touching when I sit with him. Often, he puts his paw over my hand. Then I turn my hand around to hold it. And there we are, paw in hand, staring into each other's eyes like the fools in love that we remain.

As fall gives way to winter our boy continues to thrive. Sam, though, doesn't. One morning, at five o'clock, he wakes me up. "I'm having chest pains."

I sit bolt upright. "I'm calling 911,"

"Not yet." But I don't listen to him. Literally two minutes later, six paramedics are knocking on our door. We live only a few blocks from the firehouse. At five a.m. there's no traffic. I'm barely pulling on my clothes when they get there. Chips goes nuts when three of the men get on the bed with his dad. He begins barking his head off.

"Can you do something about him?" one of the guys asks. I put Chips out of the room for a few minutes, then let him back but, hold him and say, "Shhh," putting my hand over his muzzle. This does the trick. He seems to understand that whatever is going on, he'd better behave.

After attaching electrodes to Sam's chest and asking him a few questions, the paramedics feel he isn't having a heart attack, but still want to take him to the hospital by ambulance. "We can't bring you home later," one fellow tells me. So, I follow the ambulance in my car.

In the emergency room they do a few tests and call Sam's doctor, who happens to be a cardiologist as well as an internist. The doctor decides to admit Sam for even more tests. Later that morning, I call Berta to see if she can stay with Chips while I spend most of my time at the hospital with Sam. As always, my wonderful sister-in-law takes over the care and feeding of our boy. In between my hospital visits, I come home only to walk him, pick up groceries for Berta or sleep. Chips comforts me in Sam's absence, staying on our bed much of the night, which he's never done before.

Two days later Sam returns home with no conclusion to the incident. The tests they did were all negative. He goes upstairs to take a nap, wakes up and starts to have more symptoms. We call his doctor. "I strongly recommend you go back to the emergency room." Naturally, it's Saturday night. We're both very depressed driving the two miles back to the hospital. Two more days of tests reveal that the cardio-seal they'd placed in Sam's heart three years before has grown a thrombis of some sort. The doctors have never seen, nor had the manufacturer ever heard of such a thing. Sam's cardiologist comes in with the bad news. "Sit down," he says to me while Sam is still out of the room from the last test. "This growth is very dangerous – it could break off at any moment. Sam needs to have open heart surgery to remove it."

"Are you kidding?"

"It's only attached at one corner. It could travel anywhere and kill him." I'm sure the color drained from my face. Most open heart surgery doesn't actually go inside the heart. It's really "open chest" to fix valves on the outside the heart. This operation would actually go into the heart itself. In order to remove this thing, the doctor would have to cut out the cardio-seal, which was now overgrown with Sam's own tissue. Such a surgery has never been done by anyone. A few people in the world had the seal removed a short time after insertion, but never after three years. "Dr. Trento will do it," Sam's doctor says. He assures me, "This man is one of the finest heart surgeons in the

world, with a sterling reputation and track record."
That's some comfort, but not much. I know that any
surgery, especially one so serious, poses a risk of death.
"Dr. Trento, will be coming in to talk to Sam shortly.
Would you like to see what the growth looks like on
the computer video?"

"Of course I do." The mass, attached to the small
cardio-seal, shaped like a large mushroom, is only
connected at one little corner. Every time Sam's heart
beats, the mass moves considerably. I'm surprised that
it hasn't yet broken off. I walk back to Sam's room.
After the cardiologist explains the situation to him,
we're both very quiet, each of us realizing the danger facing us, but reluctant to panic one another any
more than necessary. Dr. Trento arrives an hour later
and strikes a tone of reassurance while explaining the
operation to us in detail. Some pre-op tests will be
done the next morning and the surgery scheduled for
the day after. Nothing Dr. Trento says removes the
obvious threat to Sam's life.

Chips' problems are put on the back burner as Sam
goes through the long and difficult surgery to fix his
heart. Recuperation is not easy either, with a bout of
pneumonia adding to his post-op stay in the hospital.
After sixteen grueling days, Sam finally comes home.

Chips, who has to know something is very wrong, sticks next to his dad much of the time for the following weeks. Though he still gives me first priority, Dr. Chips ministers to his patient with obvious concern.

Weeks go by. Sam heals, and the three of us begin taking walks again, this time with me holding the leash on my left side and Sam's hand on the right. By the time spring ends Sam is doing much better, going through cardiac rehab, even though he has had none of the ailments that plague other heart patients. "His arteries," Dr. Trento told us, "...are perfect." Fairly slim, with low cholesterol, Sam had only a mechanical aberration that necessitated the surgery.

Thankfully, Sam recuperates while Chips' condition grows less stable. One terrible night the poor fellow vomits seven times. It's up and down the stairs and into the backyard again and again until the weakened little guy finally settles down. The most remarkable thing about such incidents is how he always manages to wait until he's outside. Though it requires a delay until I go down the stairs and turn off the alarm, Chips somehow makes it to our backyard each time. After the first trip, I leave the alarm off. This extraordinary control Chips displays, even when very ill, continually amazes us. It must have cost him dearly in discomfort. But Chips' natural refinement never falters.

Following that miserable night we naturally begin to think that perhaps Chips' time to leave us is here. We bring our boy in for another ultrasound with Dr. Martin, to see if the tumor has metastasized. "It's about two centimeters larger," Dr. Martin says pointing to the film, "but there is no evidence of any cancer outside the liver. "If the tumor, now twelve centimeters, just stays in the liver, even if it grows, Chips might live for some time."

"How long," I ask again.

"Hard to tell. But when you lift him, don't press on the stomach. The tumor could burst and he would bleed internally." Oh God! That sounded awful. Just imagine the guilt I'd have if I caused him to internally bleed to death. We promise to pick him up the right way. "Just enjoy him," Dr. Martin tells us again. Exactly what we were doing along with worrying constantly about Chips' comfort or lack thereof. From his behavior, and especially his tail, we judge that he still takes pleasure in life most of the time.

A dog lives totally in the present because he has no knowledge of the future. Being close to a dog forces his humans to live more of the same way, appreciating and enjoying the moment. So thanks to Chips, we're learning and really experiencing the pleasures of Now. We relish each day with him even more than before his illness, stopping more often to interact. He's become the lens though which a good part of our lives are seen, his happiness and well being determining our mood.

I think a lot about the human-dog connection. Our affinity with dogs also stems from the pattern of rituals we all have with them – sharing places we go, food, talking or singing to them, playing with, scratching, brushing them, in my case washing the feet, taking off his collar and scratching his neck... and so many other daily rituals. One doesn't normally mention these private times to anyone else because it would kind of betray the special connection between you, allowing comment or possibly belittlement by others. It is simply too important and too intimate.

The greatest gain for mankind in the dog-man connection is that we can be our truest selves with dogs, the need for diplomacy or fear of reprisal or judgment removed from the equation. The only judgment an animal makes about us depends on how he or she is treated. Dogs' affinity to us appears inborn, verified by experiments. I remember a TV program documenting some scientists raising and studying a number of puppies and wolves together from birth. The animals were treated identically by the scientists and seemed to behave alike for the first few months. But from six to twelve months, as the humans began giving all the pups directions, only the dog puppies took and tried learning the commands. The wolves simply ignored them. This distinction demonstrates the desire of dogs to please and forge a bond with people.

During Chips' illness, even more than before, those friends who welcome him to come along for an evening see more of us than the others. Likewise, we only go to restaurants which allow dogs to sit outside with their guardians. These places are always crowded. Many a chilly evening we huddle with other dog parents and our pets on a terrace or sidewalk under a few heat lamps. The customers on the outside always socialize more than the ones inside, inquiring about each other's dogs, getting into conversations and letting all the animals greet each other.

Although Chips no longer has the strength or muscles he once did, he still loves interacting with people and other dogs, walking, sometimes moving along at a good clip, with his characteristic prance and waving tail. He develops a ferocious appetite, presumably from the Artemisinin. And though kibble still isn't his favorite thing, he seems to finish it most of the time.

Amazingly, Chips makes it through his next birthday in March, '08. We always calculated his birthday as the date on which he joined the family. I bake a special meatloaf he could share. Assuming he was two when we got him, he was now thirteen. We are thrilled to still have him with us. It's been a year since diagnosis, the most the oncologist thought he would live. But despite his increased food consumption, Chips loses weight; the bones on his rump now more prominent, his muscles pretty much gone. A few weeks after his birthday, we return home from the theatre, give him his usual snack of warm baked potato and cottage cheese. After a few bites he vomits, then begins crying pathetically, as if in real pain. Accompanying this, he walks in circles, moving from one place to another – the way dogs do when they can't get comfortable. We let him out in the backyard. He tries to lie down on the grass, but immediately gets up.

My adrenalin kicks in full force. Crisis time. "Do you think the tumor has broken through the liver" I ask Sam.

"Maybe. Naturally, it's a Friday night." We have a whole weekend to go through until we can see our own very trusted vet. We know the golden rule – if a crisis happens, it's ALWAYS on a weekend. We immediately decide Chips has to go to the emergency clinic next to the cancer center, maybe get a morphine patch or shot, something to help him until we can reach our vet.

Sam's already undressed for bed. A few days before this he had broken his finger tripping over the ottoman we keep at the foot of the bed to help Chips jump up. Moving as fast as he can with his bandaged, broken finger, Sam gets into his clothes again. But by the time that we're ready to leave, Chips has stopped crying, settled down in his bed and started to fall asleep. We decide to wait a few minutes and watch him. Remarkably, our boy sleeps through the night. By the next morning he seems absolutely fine, goes for his morning walk and eats as usual. I call Dr. Martin on Monday morning to ask if we should bring Chips in. "It must have been some temporary thing like gas pains. Why don't you just watch for anything else, and let me know."

Nothing else happens but I feel positive that Chips senses something's very wrong with him because he stares into my eyes for long periods of time as if searching for answers. "I know you feel sick. I'm sorry." In the past, whenever I needed to do something uncomfortable to him, like cutting some gum he'd picked up on his paw pad, I'd say "mommy fix." He knows this means "keep still" for whatever I'm doing. Over the years he's learned, I hope, that when he lets me do these strange things, his problem improves or resolves afterwards.

If I can't fix something, like how he's feeling, I say "I'm sorry." He understands those two words from the few times he'd been hurt inadvertently. Either I caught his hair accidentally while pulling off his harness or I stepped on a paw when he jumped around me. Immediately, I apologize, sounding remorseful, pet and kiss him. So he knows at least that I understand something is wrong. Our limited communication at times like this frustrates me, but we do manage to get our messages to one another.

Amazingly, Chips holds his own until the following summer. We begin thinking of visiting our friends in Crete. But when we see Chips weakening again, our resolve disappears. During his last summer, and it no doubt was, we couldn't leave him. Instead we'll go back to Carmel for the summer months with Chips, knowing it HAS to be his last voyage up the coast. He'd already outlived all the doctors' predictions. Before leaving we have Dr. Martin do another ultrasound and find that Chips' tumor is now slightly larger than the last time. Still, miraculously, it has not metastasized outside the liver.

In Carmel, we continue Chips' walks as best we can. His pace slows significantly, but the stroller saves us. Everyone in Carmel who walks on the path above the beach knows Chips and his stroller. Naturally, the tourists still make comments – "Talk about spoiled.!" "What a life," or "You have room for me in there?" Other folks just laugh or take our picture. I simply push on, not bothering to explain anything. Remarkably, it never occurs to any one of these people that perhaps my dog is sick.

Sam and I ride an emotional rollercoaster, our moods tied more than before to Chips' condition, always broadcast by his tail. When he has a good day, I take him to Stillwater Cove. Chips still actually runs a little on the short beach. I'm determined that he'll have every shred of fun his little body can manage.

Luckily for us, we have our two veterinarian friends nearby. Both superb doctors, they aren't in private practice. The man runs a remote animal veterinary service for impoverished areas – some Indian reservations, and places in rural Latin America that have no animal medical care. His wife is the head vet in an animal shelter. We ask them if they'd be willing to help us out if Chips needs to be euthanized while we're in Carmel. Reluctantly, because of our friendship and their affection for Chips, they agree to do what's difficult for them, but might be necessary.

Fortunately for all of us, our little guy manages to get through the whole summer without their help. Once, while pushing Chips in the stroller, we meet another couple who stop to inquire about him. "Our dog died of liver cancer last year" they say. We were intensely interested, as dog people tend to be, in our common experiences.

"Did you think he had pain," I ask.

"Not really." They say that their vet also told them "When it's time, you'll just know." We'd been told the same thing by many people who'd lost pets. Comparing notes with this couple, we discover that their dog lived about a year with the cancer. Chips seems to be the record holder thus far with his seventeenth month now halfway through.

"Our dog ate until the end" they tell us.

"Gee, we were counting on food as an indication," I say.

"We were too, but our girl just got weaker and weaker," which is exactly what's happening to Chips. He wasn't any longer the great jumper he'd always been. He could still get in the car, barely, and occasionally he misses, but I'm always right behind him to help. We thank the other couple and say goodbye.

My back suddenly starts acting up for the first time since surgery. After weeks of intermittent pain I discover that it's from incorrectly picking Chips up and putting him in the stroller. I try doing it exactly as the surgeon told me to, from a crouching position, after hugging Chips against me, but it's almost impossible to get up from this position. Sam fares no better at it. One day I wonder if, before pulling up the stroller to an upright position, Chips would be capable of getting onto the seat while it's still folded. That would eliminate the need to pick him up. Or, maybe when I pull it up, he'll be dumped out. We need to try it once. I guide Chips over and ask him to "come" toward the seat. He does and gets in. Then I pull the stroller up to a standing position. Voila! It works perfectly, and I don't have to lift him. What a great dog. This becomes our new routine. My back returns to its delightfully pain-free mode.

One afternoon, at high tide, after letting Chips off the leash at Stillwater Cove, I'm walking behind him when I spot some large animal halfway down the beach. It looks like a sea lion, sitting in front of the rocks which jut out in front of the water. The only sand at that point is completely occupied by the animal. While Chips heads that way, it occurs to me that the sea lion might not welcome the friendship of a dog. I just don't know. I'm not taking any chances, though Chips definitely wants to continue down the beach.

"Chips come!," I quickly call. He looks confused because we've just gotten here, but he must hear something in my voice as I repeat the words. He turns around and trots back to me. When we meet I hook his leash on the harness, wishing that I had my camera with me. I'm not sure how close we can get but know it's necessary to pass the seal to continue down the small beach. The larger animal looks quite copacetic, sunning himself as he faces the beach. But just as we reach him he makes a small move toward us. I place myself between Chips and the seal as the larger animal suddenly barks at us, lunging a little. Right afterward, he moves off into the water. As we round the jutting rock we see a man, his wife and small daughter, with their two Golden Retrievers standing against the wall of vegetation away from the water.

"We've been trying to get by him for ten minutes, but he wouldn't let us," the husband says. "Thanks." I realize they're obviously smarter than I to have been fearful.

"Do seals attack people" I ask.

"I don't know." A moment after the family leaves, two women walking a Sheepdog and a mixed breed, come toward us. The one with the Sheepdog informs me that seals indeed attack dogs when they're in the water. "They pull them under."

"Then what?"

"They eat them."

"What? I thought they only ate fish."

"Apparently not. I know someone who lost his dog that way." Wow. Imagine the nightmares and guilt I'd have if that had happened. Thank God Chips was securely next to me. After the sea lion swims far out of sight, I let my boy off the leash again knowing he'd never go in the water. He stays fairly close, perhaps sensing there might be danger lurking. In fact, I do see the sea lion come up very high onto the rocks further down the beach, on the other side of the pier, exactly where Chips is headed, but in an area that's inaccessible to him and way above his line of sight. The almost black seal, camouflaged by the rocks, can barely be seen . When we reach the pier, Chips wants to go on the shorter side of the beach, but I call him back. He's obedient, probably because I give him so few commands. He comes immediately and follows me up the four broad steps to the parking area.

That night, Chips stretches himself out on Sam's side of the bed before I get in my side. He's already sleeping when Sam comes to bed. My husband, adoring this little creature, looks down at Chips. "I will not disturb him. The poor guy is dying. He's finally sleeping on our bed, after eleven and a half years. I'm not going to move him." And Sam picks up his pillow and goes to the other small bedroom because Chips always wants to sleep where I am. I kiss Sam goodnight knowing there are few other men in the world like him.

For much of the summer, Chips seems his normal but weaker self, though once he has breathing problems for about five minutes. He still manages his marathon begging in the stores of Carmel. One morning we run into a man we know walking his German Shepard, Mack. We talk about Chips' continuing but slow downhill slide. He tells us, "Mack has recently been sick with chronic diarrhea. After visits to several vets, none of whom could cure him, we went to see a lady named Sarah at a pet food store in the Barnyard." In a local shopping area the store is called The Raw Connection. "She suggested putting Mack on cooked pumpkin and raw meat, which they sell in dehydrated and frozen versions at the store." The meat was frozen or dried immediately after the animal of origin was killed. Our acquaintance went along with this plan of eating. "Two days later Mack's diarrhea was gone and has never returned." Needless to say this information piqued our interest.

We make a visit to Sarah. It brings a revelation – she listens, then tells us, "It's important to get Chips off the kibble and any other carbohydrates he's eating. They're known to promote cancer growth." This idea is a complete reversal from the theory in the book "The China Syndrome." I don't know if the carbohydrate problem is valid just for dogs or people too. A few customers in the store that day and a pet food company president confirm that they know this information about cancer and have read several books on it. Sam and I are stunned. If this theory is true then we'd been feeding Chips all the wrong stuff for a long time. He ate both kibble and other things containing carbohydrates. We'd found his medicine, Artemisi-nin, outside the medical establishment, so why not give this a try?

We buy bags of frozen and dehydrated raw meats and fish. They're much easier to use than the earlier incarnation of raw meat we had once bought for Chips. The dehydrated chicken and lamb burgers could be given as is or mixed with water. Another dehydrated powdered mixture requires boiled water. Chips loves everything we offer as samples in the store. Sarah wants us to add raw vegetables to the food we buy.

Now we cut out all the carbs, including the kib-ble Chips had been doing well on, but doesn't really like. He gobbles down the new, no doubt tastier, mor-sels the first week. Within a short time, his tolerance for this very concentrated raw protein grows thin. He seems to want his old cookies, but I just give him the pure protein new ones. In front or inside a few stores in Carmel are bowls of small Milk Bone dog biscuits – Chips finds them irresistible. He looks at me when he sees them. I immediately whip out a protein treat to lure him away, but that doesn't work. I eventually allow him to have one of the Milk Bones. How can you refuse a terminally ill cancer patient a cookie he wants, especially if you can't explain the reason to refuse?

I try to order some more Artemisinin, but the lab we'd used is apparently out of business. My next call is to the doctors at the University of Washington. The doctor I hadn't spoken to before answered the phone. He tells me about Artemix, a stronger and superior pill to the one I'd been giving Chips, and provides the information to order it. He also says, "The results continue to be excellent, but we've had no luck selling our compound to a pharmaceutical company."

"Why?"

"There's nothing patentable." I realize that because all the ingredients are natural, no pharmaceutical company can maintain a hold on the formula and therefore wouldn't want to invest money in marketing it. This research doctor tells me "I take the pill myself, for my own cancer, and am doing quite well." I think of all the wonderful, natural products and compounds that might help all of us, which are not being brought to market for just such reasons.

Sam needs a day in L.A. to take care of a few things. He goes by plane and will be flying back to Monterey Airport this evening. Having a good morning, Chips, I decide, might like a visit to the little beach at Stillwater Cove. Recently, he'd not been doing well enough to walk down to and up from the beach. Once there, he gets excited as we head for the sand. I remove his leash on the second step down – he trots the rest of the way, then runs, although much slower than in former days, down the beach. My heart does a little jig as I watch him make his way along the sand, tail waving, glancing back every few yards. He looks happy, so happy. I take off my sandals and walk the sand with him.

Together we go along, Chips out front closer to the water, even getting his paws wet now and again, a bold foray for a dog who prefers to be dry. Two thirds of the way down the beach, Chips stops, raises his head and barks, kind of howling in joy. I smile. "Yes, it's great!" I have tears in my eyes with gratitude for this moment. The beach is just long enough to have a good walk and short enough that Chips can still manage it. Halfway back he raises his head again and barks triumphantly. Ergo, my spirits soar. What a memorable day. Delighted to be with Chips in our cocoon, I only wish that Sam were here to share it.

Chapter 29

TWO PERFECT POOPS

*We are alone, absolutely alone on this chance
planet; and amid all the forms of life that surround
us, not one, excepting the dog, has made an
alliance with us.*

MAETERLINCK

By the fall of '08, life with Chips has become an
even more difficult emotional rollercoaster, rendering
Sam and I completely limp. We feel rung out by the
daily ups and downs of Chips' condition. We waver
and wonder about his possible suffering and quality of
life – an awesome responsibility. Our friends and family, who don't live with him, see him as o.k. because, I
presume, he still walks around in our house and some
short distances outside. Actually, the bounce always

present in his walk, remarkably, usually still appears. He isn't lying in a corner or crying, signs some people need to admit that a dog is really sick. But Chips has lost a significant amount of weight, despite Dr. Martin's suggested five daily feedings. The vertebrae and bones in his lower back stick up prominently.

Our boy's bad days are intermittent. We have become tailgaters, constantly watching his curved plume to see if it's wagging or drooping. Our friends take to calling Chips the Energizer Bunny because he just keeps going. After a particularly successful walk, I come back feeling victorious and announce to Sam, who genuinely wants to know these things, "two perfect poops!"

Sam smiles. "Hey, Chips, you're a great dog!" Both of us smile a lot when his stomach seems stable. When it isn't, Dr. Martin gets a call. As the months go by, I call him more often, sometimes daily. Instead of growing tired of all my calls, Dr. Martin unfailingly returns them the same day, patiently suggesting tweaking Chips' food or routines to make his life better.

At the same time, we watch our beloved boy struggling up the stairs, sort of pulling his back half more with his front right leg. By the time he reaches the landing, he's out of breath. Nonetheless, he wants to follow me as usual. When I know that I'm going upstairs for just a moment to get something, I discourage him from trailing after me, thinking to preserve his strength. "Stay. I come right back," I tell him. He knows what that means. But if I take any longer than Chips deems necessary, there he goes, slowly pulling himself up those eighteen stone steps. The difficulty of deciding what to do weighs more heavily on me each day. I realize that keeping him downstairs by means of a baby gate at the foot of the stairs would be even harder on him emotionally than the challenge of getting upstairs is physically. He just doesn't want to be separated from me. This need goes way beyond what it was before the cancer. I do, however, use the gate intermittently.

Chips still enjoys going out with us. Isn't that the most emblematic and significant thing? To be with? I always, always do try to take him, even when inconvenient, even when he's slow – anything to see his face light up. Of course, his weakness necessitates leaving him at home more and more. I hate it. We invite people over if we cannot bring him to their places, and only go to really important events. What, we ask ourselves, is another dinner at a restaurant or a movie compared to a night with Chips?

Thank God for that black and white tail – its thumping the only signal that he's not totally lost, despite the sad face on the floor part of the time. His spirit still comes through – some measure of joy and an expression of love remaining. At night, Chips needs to go to sleep earlier than normal. When we see him heading toward the stairs, we often take ourselves up, because he won't go without us. I also find myself staying in bed past the hour of wakefulness because I don't want to disturb his much needed sleep. The moment I get out of bed, no matter how carefully or quietly, Chips wakes up as soon as I stir, and pulls himself out too.

We notice another change -- Chips goes to great effort to drink water from his pottery dish in our bedroom, often dragging himself all the way upstairs just to do this. We always leave it filled with water in the bedroom so that he won't have to go down and into the kitchen when he's thirsty at night. This past year he's been adamant about drinking from that dish only, going to it even during the day. Naturally, I wonder what the reason could be; the dishes in the kitchen are also pottery. I replaced the metal bowls that came with his "table" after I saw that my prince preferred the pottery ones. Puzzling over his new habit a while, I finally understand his preference. With the smaller bowl, his "beard" does not get wet while he drinks. The larger bowl leaves it soaking wet. Mr. Refinement prefers to stay neat and dry.

Chips now actually sleeps part of every night on our bed. Remarkably, he still manages to jump on the ottoman at the foot and then up onto the mattress. I marvel at this, but even more so at his sensitivities, given his grave condition. Each night begins with him lying at the foot of our bed. The moment either Sam or I start to get into it, he moves over to the side opposite to make room for the feet of the first human occupant. Apparently, Chips must realize that we try not to put our feet where he's lying. But we can't keep our feet away from the foot of the bed all night, although, given the treatment he's used to, he might expect that.

We try huddling right next to each other in the middle unless Chips moves. Strangely, he stays on one side or the other, never in the middle, where there would be a perfect space for him. If I place him there, he moves back to one side or the other. We struggle to avoid kicking or disturbing him during the night because any movement that can be interpreted as rejection, he's off instantly.

Much of the time now, a melancholy, perhaps from nausea, reflects in Chips' face. But is that enough to put a dog to sleep? I don't know the answer. We continuously question ourselves about whether we're doing right by him. During the day, he still lies in my office with his head on the floor between his front paws. His body continues to weaken, the back legs slipping around when he tries to move quickly over the wooden surface. But still there are times when he "smiles" at us, that little face lighting up at our arrival home and when, I imagine, he feels better. The ceaselessly wagging tail, however, that elicited so much comment during his better days, has vanished. The black and white emblem moves back and forth only when I talk to him, and then only some of the time. He fusses more about food, rejecting many things he used to love, and now and then needs hand feeding to start him off.

Two nights ago I was organizing our photos, and came across one of Chips at the Pebble Beach Lodge with his canine friends, Aspen, a Golden Retriever, and Lady Jane, a Cavalier King Charles. Lady Jane has died less than two months ago. I know that Aspen is very old, almost sixteen, unheard of for a Golden. I wonder which of the surviving canines will be next to "cross the rainbow bridge," as they say.

One week after finding that photo, our friend, Gloria, calls to tell us, "We had to put Aspen down yesterday." I know that their dog hasn't been well the last two weeks, but didn't realize things had reached the end point. Our friends are devastated, of course. I wonder when Chips will follow Aspen. He no longer takes the almond butter he loves, a great vehicle to hide pills. Peanut butter is no better, nor cheese. I'm left with no way to give him the large Artemix pills. The pet store carries something called "pill pockets" a treat most dogs love. I buy and offer them to Chips. He turns up his nose. I cannot open the capsules and sprinkle the medicine on his food because the doctors who created it said that the stuff is exceedingly bitter. I will not ruin Chips' only remaining pleasure, food, by covering it in bitter medicine.

Formerly our four legged wonder almost flew out the door heading for the car, clearing the seat by inches as he leapt inside. Now he walks there slowly, looking daunted at the prospect of having to jump into the car. I want to lift him up, but don't want to ruin my surgery. As weak as Chips remains, he, remarkably, still manages a jump into the car. But he plans and calculates those jumps slowly, starting from a distance and getting a bit of momentum going with his front legs first. When we go out, I take Sam's old sports car, which I don't like driving, but it's low to the ground and a much easier jump for Chips than my sedan. I stand behind him ready with a boost if he needs it.

One night, Chips appears to have trouble breathing again. His movements are an exaggeration of what Dr. Martin has called "reverse sneezing," but this incident seems worse and lasts longer. The following day, Dr. Martin gets another visit, and does an x-ray of Chips' lungs to see if the cancer has metastasized. It hasn't. Miraculously, the liver tumor looks unchanged from the last ultrasound. "He's still doing well" Dr. Martin says.

"And we'll know when it's time," we ask again.

"Yes you will." Chips begins skipping meals here and there. At Dr. Martin's suggestion we are feeding him small portions more often. If he doesn't want what I give him, I try something else. Frequently, it works. Lamb chops are his favorite thing.

Occasionally, Chips wakes up like a new dog, tail wagging, eyes bright, demeanor cheerful. Our hearts are full. We can't understand how he's managing, but we're thrilled. Everyone keeps saying "you'll know when it's time. He'll tell you." I have a sense that many people wait until it's so obvious that the animal must be really suffering. That is something Sam and I promise not to let Chips do. I often think of Yeats'

poem, Sailing to Byzantium, about our souls being "…
tied to a dying animal." I observe Chips' plight and
all the human bodies' weaknesses overcoming beloved
relatives or friends every year. I am positive that if we
have souls, then animals certainly do. One day I see
Chips staring at the wall. "They do that shortly before
they die," Sam tells me.

"Where did you hear this?"

"I've known that for a long time." Though I'm sure
that the time for parting is near, this information
makes me very sad. I'm not positive it's true as Sam
carries a few other superstitions he'd learned in Cuba,
like not placing new shoes on the bed. Otherwise, bad
luck will follow. So, I don't know how much stock to
put into this wall thing. Of course we won't let Chips
die naturally. When he gets to the point where he's
sick enough to die soon, we would have him put to
sleep to spare him further discomfort.

Friends who've been through this awful event tell
us "it was one of the worse days of my life. It's horrible." In fact my dentist, a wonderful man, took his
dog to the vet when the time came, but had to wait in
the reception area while the doctor in back gave his
dog the shot to put him into the sleep state that they
do before the fatal shot. My dentist didn't realize that

the dog would be comatose by the time he went in. Although the incident happened a few years ago, he still feels cheated out of saying goodbye to his pet, a terrible thing for both of them.

Chapter 30

GOODBYE MR. CHIPS

Beneath this spot are deposited the remains of a being Who was possessed of beauty without vanity, Strength without insolence, Courage without ferocity, And all the virtues of man without his vices.

BYRON

We are determined to make Chips' end of life the best we can. Our friend Marjorie gives us the name of a vet who comes to your house to "put the dog to sleep." Our own vets, with one of the largest practices in the area, are simply too busy to go to people's houses. But saying goodbye to Chips at home is exactly what we want.

Dr. Kelly came over for an interview shortly after Chips got diagnosed with cancer. She seemed gentle with our dog and understanding, explaining precisely what she would do when he was ready. But a few months later, maternity leave made Dr. Kelly unavailable. Sam and I worried about who we would call when the time came. But the year and a half went by with Chips mostly well. Around Thanksgiving of '08 we interview another woman vet who makes the same kind of house calls as Dr. Kelly. Chips eyes her suspiciously, we think, then realize it might be the smell of other dogs on her clothing which tips him off to a vet lurking around his house.

Christmas and the New Year come and go. I do notice Chips staring at walls several times. By January we are pretty much going day to day, staying at home even more than usual to do what we can for him. I call Nancy from Perfect Pet Rescue, who comes over to see Chips a final time. Dr. Kelly, we've heard, is now back from maternity leave.

Sam and I weigh Chips' condition daily. Was his life worth living anymore? The truth – we simply don't know. One day, in the middle of January, I go out with Chips' leash in my hand, expecting him to follow as always. After walking through the front door, Chips just stands in the driveway while I walk toward the car. "Come on Pumpkin Pie." But he just stands there, tail drooping, staring at me. I walk over, kneel down and pet him. "You don't have to go walking if you don't want to." I stand up and follow him back into the house. This is the very first time in twelve years that he has not wanted to go on an outing. Sam and I discuss what happened. "It's a sign."

"You're right. He must feel really bad."

I know now that Chips' time to leave us is close. Although he goes out for his walks the following day, about a week later, he again wants to stay home. Sam and I now feel the time is probably right for us to call Dr. Kelly. Chips clearly will not begin crying or stop eating until he is in a really bad crisis. We don't want to get to that point. His hanging tail tells us that life holds no joy for him anymore. If we put him to sleep a little bit too soon, it is preferable to too late. The exact perfect time is impossible for us to know. But either way, it's still excruciating. We have shared not just the predictable, presentable, moments, but times of the most painful and touching intimacies, the least graceful notes and nuances.

I should have had a dog during past illnesses or at times of romantic breakups. I never realized how much the solitary life of a writer could have been enhanced by the presence of a dog. The simplicity of their trust, goodness and unambivalent love creates a relationship that makes life much richer. We call Dr. Kelly to come over and discuss the procedure again. She explains once more in detail how she would put Chips to sleep with a shot. "It will take a few minutes to work. You could say goodbye to him then. And when he's definitely out, I give him the intravenous shot which will stop his heart."

I stop breathing while she describes this. Chips is doing a little better today. I know that Sam and I need a bit more time to make up our minds about the moment being right. "Call anytime," Dr. Kelly tells us before she leaves.

The only thing worse than putting your dog to sleep is letting him suffer. We feel we know by Chips' face and tail that he feels lousy, probably nauseous, if not in pain. The following day, he eats his lamb chop and vegetables, though I have to hand feed him. A cooked egg, which he never has turned down, is left in his plate that night. The next morning he wants nothing. This is IT. We bring his Aunt Berta over to visit Chips one more time. Later that day we make the call to Dr. Kelly. She'll come in the afternoon. She suggests I call the pet mortuary. "They come over and pick him up, then cremate him. They're wonderful," she says. We had decided to cremate Chips because burying seems too risky. Who knows how many years we'll live in our house? With ashes, we can always make up our minds what to do with them later on.

Ironically, Chips will eat nothing after I make that call, not even a cut up lamb chop or his favorite cookie from my hand. It's January 22nd, a sunny day. Chips sits outside with me while I tell him what a terrific guy he is. Sam remains extremely quiet. I turn on classical music and we nervously await the doctor. "Better that we outlive him then the other way around" I say. Sam nods in agreement. I know that putting Chips to sleep is the right thing to do, but wish there were another way out.

The bell rings. Chips barks, as always. Dr. Kelly comes in. "Hi. Hello Chips." There are not many pleasantries exchanged. We've come together for a solemn occasion. I take Chips on my lap and hold him close, kiss his head, as does Sam. Dr. Kelly stands behind Chips and administers a shot. Chips yelps and jumps out of my arms, a look of mistrust crossing his face. That yelp cuts through Sam and me. We didn't think it would be painful. "I barely touched him. It doesn't hurt," Dr. Kelly says. Well, obviously Chips disagrees with that.

I wish he hadn't suffered that pinch as his last memory. He walks over near the French doors and lies down. Sam and I sit down to pet him and tell him again that we love him. Slowly, his head starts to bob a little and his eyes blink until they close for the last time. A few moments later, he's definitely asleep. I pick him up and sit on the ottoman with him in my lap. We both kiss him again. "I have to shave some hair, but he definitely can't feel this," Dr. Kelly assures us, using a clipper on his leg. She follows this with the intravenous injection. Chips' heart beats against my arm for another few moments. Then it stops. Just like that. Chips is gone from us.

Naturally, Sam and I begin dissolving while Dr. Kelly gathers her things together. Another car pulls into the driveway. No one has to tell me it's the man from the mortuary. I hold Chips' small body, but am not ready to relinquish him as yet. Sam and I sit there for another few minutes while the man in the car stays outside. Dr. Kelly leaves. Finally, Sam opens the door and waves to the guy. Carrying a small box lined with plastic, the fellow puts it down in our living room and I place Chips inside. It seems tacky to put him in plastic, but it's understandable.

"They'll deliver the ashes and a certificate in a few days," he says. And then he's gone.

Sam and I feel utterly bereft and know that we need to leave the house immediately. We go for a walk in town, zombie like, wandering we know not where. "The only good thing about losing him is knowing that he won't have to live without us," I tell Sam.

Suddenly, our friend, Jim, the manager of Brooks Brothers, appears before us about a block from his store. He smiles broadly. "Hi. Where's Chips?" Whenever we'd gone to Brooks Brothers, Chips had been with us. We tell him what we've just done. He commiserated for a few minutes.

"We're both wrecks" I say.

"I think I'm just about ready to get a dog myself. And it's been a couple of years." I suggest he call Perfect Pet Rescue, where we'd found Chips.

"I want a Miniature Schnauzer again." Jim had had one of that breed before. I was confident I'd find him a rescue Schnauzer, but didn't think it likely that Nancy had one. They're just not that common to find.

"I'm sure there's one around who needs a good home." I call Nancy when I get back, thinking that she might know who to call next. "Chips is gone," I tell her, then mention our friend's interest in a Miniature Schnauzer.

"Believe it or not, I just picked one up few hours ago," she says.

"You're kidding?"

"No, really." It sounds crazy that the very breed he mentioned suddenly dropped into the local rescue group's lap, so to speak. I call Jim at his store.

"Perfect Pet Rescue just got a Miniature Schnauzer a half hour ago." A few days later, Jim goes, sees and adopts Zak, the name he gives his new best friend.

I launder Chips' donut bed and take it over to Brooks Brothers. Jim thanks me for it and has since reported on Zack's approval. "Sometimes he even drags it through his doggy door to the backyard." I'm so glad that something of Chips' has another incarnation. I also bring his large, square, orthopedic cushion over to Koko. She needs something in the kitchen area.

"She won't sit on it" my friend Paula reports a week later. Although I had washed the removable covering, perhaps Chips' scent remains on the inner foam rubber part. Maybe Koko recognizes the scent and doesn't want to get on Chips' cushion.

"Maybe, just get her a new cushion of her own," I suggest. Only one consolation remains after surrendering Chips to the inevitable –– we have done the very best we could for him. I could not say that about every single loved one I've lost, but in Chips' case it was true. In addition to our few regrets we console ourselves with the knowledge that he no longer suffered. The former responsibility of deciding whether his life was still worth living had been an awful burden.

Condolence cards, letters and contributions in Chips' memory begin coming every day in the mail for weeks. They touch us deeply. In fact, I receive more cards and letters for Chips demise than I did after the death of my mother, father and brother combined. But then Chips knew more of our friends than did my family members on the East Coast. For a long time, I find poop bags in my jacket pockets. Several months after Chips left us, our friend and his, Dr. Ted Goldstein, gave us a beautiful, framed, photographic portrait that he made of Chips from a spontaneous picture he'd taken in his own kitchen. We are bowled over. Ted is a superb photographer and develops his own pictures. It hangs in our foyer where it greets us every time we come home. A miniature version of that photo is on the front cover of this book.

Eventually, I give away all of Chips' toys, treats, food and his car bed to a local rescue organization.

His nicest raincoat went to Ruben's dog, Georgie, but certain of his things, a red sweater and washable suede coat, I have kept. Holding onto them makes me feel that some small part of him remains with us. After all, our connections to dogs and people we love matter, and make up part of who we become.

A week after Chips' dies, his ashes arrive in a beautiful box with a poem and his footprint baked in clay. He has been, I realize, my Lifetime Dog. In Jon Katz's book, *A Good Dog* (New York: Villard, 2006), he talks about Lifetime dogs being those who "...intersect with our lives with particular impact; they're dogs we love in especially powerful, sometimes inexplicable ways. While we may cherish other pets, we may never feel that particular kind of connection with any of the rest. For lack of a better term, they are dogs we fall in love with..." Chips certainly was such a dog for me. He was the one with whom I was my most genuine self – filled often with delight and once in a while with profound sadness. He made me more than I would have been without him, and I know that Sam feels the same way. Dogs bring out our truest selves, whatever they may be.

I look around our house. No more towels cover the light colored furniture. Everything appears as it was designed to. The ottoman Sam once tripped over in the bedroom has been shoved back to the chair in the corner. Toys, brushes, beds, cushions and dishes once left on the floor no longer need to be walked around. Neatness and order prevail, but there's no pleasure in that. I wish I had every unmatched towel, doggy cushion and leash messing up our rooms. Whenever the doorbell rings I still expect the loud barking that has followed this sound for twelve years.

Coming home to silence is a dour experience that all former dog parents know. But if, as we all hope, there is something beyond this earthly place we share, I know that Sam and I will be reunited with each other and Chips. There, on some ideal beach, he'll be running along the sea, barking at the immutable rolling waves and howling for joy, Sam and I tagging behind, trying to keep up with him.

THE DOG AND US

I think about the idea that dogs communicate with us but cannot speak in a language that we share. Their obvious desire to have more interchange makes us sympathize with them in unique ways. The poet, W.H. Auden, wrote "Talking to Dogs" in which he captures their listening quality so well – "Being quicker to sense unhappiness without having to be told the dreary details or who is to blame, in dark hours your silence may be of more help than many two-legged comforters." So true.

Domestic dogs need our help and love, which compel us to care for them. And they are worthy of the sacrifices we make to do so. A world unto themselves, they have to live in ours because we've put them here.

They witness our lives and try to do our bidding, to please us; likewise, compassionate guardians try to fulfill their pets' needs and desires.

No doubt that our connections to dogs and cats matter, making us understand more of the universe. And this intimacy between our species goes back many millennia. In fact, dogs were the first species to be brought into intimate contact with man. An archaeological excavation in Israel revealed a man buried with his dog about 12,000 years ago. (Marjorie Garber,*DOG LOVE*, New York: Simon and Schuster,1996) The fact that they were considered appropriate companions for human journeys to eternity reveals a lot about the relationship with dogs that has never existed with other animals. People often hide the intensity of their feelings toward their dogs or cats – it's considered more "normal" to talk of children in this way, but not pets. For many of us, though, ersatz children are what they are.

A few weeks after Chips left this world, Sam and I casually talk about selling our house and buying a more rural place so we can adopt not one, but many rescue dogs. Having just one dog, of course, makes it easier to take him or her to more places like stores, outdoor areas of restaurants and on trips. "But two provide company for each other when they're left," Sam says.

We mull all this over. Chips will always be part of who we've become. Right now we are just catching our breath and taking some of the trips we delayed. But there will be another dog or dogs, definitely from a shelter, in the not too distant future. Until then, volunteering to help animal rescue groups and maybe fostering rescued animals in our area will have to suffice.

At present our country and the world creep slowly, oh so slowly, toward improving the lives of dogs and other animals over whom we have dominion. People who never paid attention to animal protection issues had their attention riveted on the extreme cruelty of dog fighting by the Michael Vick case. Until then, many were unaware of how prevalent this horrible practice is among inner city youth, gang members and others. Also, several states are currently trying to outlaw and pass much stricter laws about "puppy mills," the unspeakably cruel places that produce almost all dogs filling pet stores. Why can't we just outlaw breeding altogether, until there are no more dogs and cats to be adopted? As it is, millions of them are put to death in shelters every year for no reason other than no one came to adopt them.

Many people do not neuter their dogs and cats, producing even more animals for adoption. There simply aren't enough people to take care of this many animals.

The world, at least in Western civilization, puts dogs at the forefront of animal consideration. But for each pampered pooch around, there are thousands of homeless and abused dogs, cats, chimps and various other animals under the control of man-not-so-kind.

Not long ago, a magazine, "Coastal Canine," came to my attention. It's one of the many new magazines popping up to cater to dog "owners" – offering ads for pet massages, laser treatments, pet portraits, grief counseling for mourning pet parents and day care options by the dozens. On the one hand, as a society, we are treating our beloved pets with more and better options while allowing, actually encouraging the perpetuation of ever more dogs that are suffering their whole lives in wire cages, breeding unspeakable numbers of dogs that some people buy, the latest trend being designer mixes like Labradoodles or derivatives like Havanese. Presumably, people have discovered that mixes are often healthier than purebreds. And now even these new dogs are showing up at shelters as increased housing foreclosures, economic hardships and hurricanes cause more homelessness. The result is that millions of healthy dogs and cats of all types are being left and are waiting for adoption in shelters and rescue groups all over the country. Many of the ones in shelters will be killed if no one adopts them.

Domestic pet care has trended upward in the thirteen years since we adopted Chips. Some dog "owners," if they can manage it, may provide greater resources for the pets who still have homes. In dog food alone, you can choose among raw, dehydrated, organic, vegetarian, holistic and vegan food. Kibble comes in a dizzying array of flavors.

One issue of "Los Angeles" magazine (May, 2010) features a pet guide with information about boarding, feeding, training, grooming and socializing Fido. Restaurants with dog menus pop up monthly in various cities, particularly in California. One owned by raw food advocates is "Pussy and Pooch Pethouse and Pawbar" in Long Beach. They installed a low bar to introduce raw food to their canine visitors. Explaining that the animals behave as in a Hollywood nightclub, Guido, one of the owners, said "Things get sloppier as the night progresses. Water gets spilled, the place gets trashed, and humping does go on. Fights break out; patrons get ejected."

Agility also appears to be currently more available in Los Angeles than it was during Chips' life. The guide in L.A. magazine lists a place only forty minutes away from where we live. It also lists swimming, sheep-herding and, believe it or not, snake avoidance classes for dogs. I should take that one myself. And my pre-diction about money to be made by the airlines has come to fruition with at least one company – Pet Air. Exclusively transporting pets without their guardians, they at least are dedicated to safely and humanely fly-ing the dogs in the main cabin of their planes.

I know that most people who have pets today view them as members of the family and do whatever they can manage for them. This sometimes prompts criti-cism from others who never think to disapprove of spending money on the arts or oversized TVs or luxury cars. But times are achanging – no Christmas fam-ily photo excludes the family pet anymore and many vacations don't either, especially as more hotels wise up to the increased business gained from welcoming four-legged customers.

More than many other areas of our lives, pets and our treatment of them demonstrate our values, both as a nation and as individuals. Our dominion over these creatures thrusts a responsibility on us that is not unlike that for our children. Although we use these animals for service or protection and, recently, even more canine talents have been discovered with cancer sniffing dogs providing accurate diagnoses for patients, we usually want them merely to love and be loved. Even in hospitals and nursing homes, dogs and cats provide such emotional connections either by their live-in presence or visits with their guardians. Finally, I hope, we are learning these animals' true worth.

17501873R00201

Made in the USA
Lexington, KY
14 September 2012